#수능독해첫걸음
#내가바로독해강자

바로 읽는
배경지식 독해

Chunjae
Makes
Chunjae

[바로 읽는 배경지식 독해] LEVEL 3

기획총괄	장경률
편집개발	김윤미, 김희윤, 이민선
디자인총괄	김희정
표지디자인	윤순미, 안채리
내지디자인	디자인뮤제오
제작	황성진, 조규영

발행일	2022년 5월 15일 2판 2022년 5월 15일 1쇄
발행인	(주)천재교육
주소	서울시 금천구 가산로9길 54
신고번호	제2001-000018호
고객센터	1577-0902
교재 내용문의	(02)3282-8834

중학부터 시작하는 수능 독해 첫걸음

바로 읽는 배경지식 독해

LEVEL 3

Draw Your Future Name Card ✏

Picture Here

My Name _____

My Job _____

How to Use

영어 독해를 잘하기 위해서는 단순히 영어 문장만 읽을 줄 안다고 해서 다 되는 것이 아닙니다.
영어 문장을 읽어도 도무지 무슨 말인지 모르는 경우가 많기 때문입니다.

바로 읽는 배경지식 독해 시리즈는 여러분의 독해 실력 향상을 위해 다음과 같이 구성하였습니다.

배경지식 (Background Knowledge)	+	어휘 (Vocabulary)

이 책을 통해 배경지식과 어휘 실력을 키워 나간다면,
수능 영어에서 출제되는 다양한 주제의 글들도 쉽게 이해할 수 있습니다.

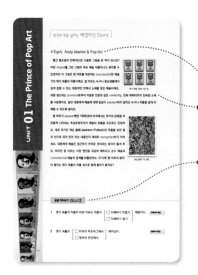

생각의 폭을 넓히는 배경지식 Story

- 재미있는 이야기를 통해, 주제에 관해 미리 생각해 보고 독해를 준비합니다.

- 읽을수록 어휘 실력도 향상됩니다. 잘 모르는 어휘는 Vocabulary에서 확인합니다.

- 본문 미리보기 QUIZ 를 통해 배울 내용을 간단한 퀴즈로 미리 만나보세요.

독해의 장벽을 깨는 만만한 Vocabulary

- 본문에 나오는 15개의 어휘를 미리 학습합니다.

- QR코드 제공: native speaker의 음성으로 단어를 들어보세요.

- 어휘 자신만만 QUIZ 를 통해 실력을 간단히 체크합니다.

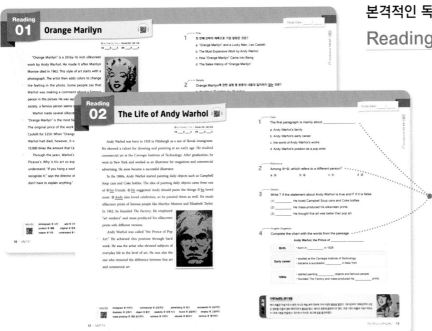

본격적인 독해 실력 향상을 위한

Reading 01, 02

1개의 Unit이 통합교과적 연관성을 지닌 두 개의 재미있는 이야기로 구성되어 있습니다.

● 체계적인 독해를 위한 main idea → details → summary 등과 같은 문제로 구성되어 있습니다.

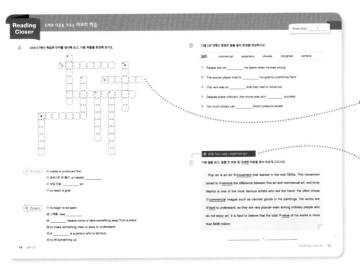

독해의 내공을 키우는 마무리 학습

Unit에서 배운 어휘를 종합 점검합니다.

● crossword puzzle을 통한 재미있는 어휘 학습을 합니다.

🔆 **생각을 키우는 서술형 · 수행평가 대비 훈련**

앞에서 배운 2개의 Reading을 종합적으로 이해 및 평가합니다. 서술형 쓰기 연습을 통해 다양한 종류의 시험을 대비합니다.

실력 향상 WORKBOOK

각 Reading마다 실력 향상을 위한 워크북이 제공됩니다.

● 쉬운 독해를 위한 Vocabulary와 끊어 읽기 구문 학습으로 여러분의 독해 실력을 한층 더 업그레이드할 수 있습니다.

Table of Contents

Background Knowledge Reading

Self Study Management Table 자기 주도 학습 관리표

Unit	Start 공부 시작		Finish 공부 끝		Self Check 배경지식을 많이 쌓았어요!			어휘 실력이 늘었어요!			독해에 자신감이 +1 늘었어요!			모든 문제들을 다 풀었어요!			My Comment 내 자신에게 한 마디!
01	월	일	월	일	☺	☺	☹	☺	☺	☹	☹	☺	☹	☹	☺	☹	
02	월	일	월	일	☺	☺	☹	☺	☺	☹	☹	☺	☹	☺	☺	☹	
03	월	일	월	일	☹	☺	☹	☺	☺	☹	☹	☺	☹	☹	☺	☹	
04	월	일	월	일	☹	☺	☹	☹	☺	☹	☹	☺	☹	☹	☺	☹	
05	월	일	월	일	☺	☺	☹	☺	☺	☹	☺	☺	☹	☹	☺	☺	
06	월	일	월	일	☹	☺	☹	☺	☺	☺	☹	☺	☹	☹	☺	☹	
07	월	일	월	일	☹	☺	☹	☹	☺	☹	☹	☺	☹	☹	☺	☹	
08	월	일	월	일	☺	☺	☹	☺	☺	☹	☺	☺	☹	☹	☺	☹	
09	월	일	월	일	☺	☺	☹	☺	☺	☹	☺	☺	☹	☹	☺	☹	
10	월	일	월	일	☺	☺	☹	☹	☺	☹	☹	☺	☹	☹	☺	☺	
11	월	일	월	일	☺	☺	☹	☹	☺	☹	☺	☺	☹	☺	☺	☹	
12	월	일	월	일	☺	☺	☹	☹	☺	☹	☹	☺	☹	☺	☺	☹	
13	월	일	월	일	☹	☺	☹	☺	☺	☹	☹	☺	☹	☺	☺	☹	
14	월	일	월	일	☹	☺	☹	☹	☺	☹	☹	☺	☹	☺	☺	☹	
15	월	일	월	일	☺	☺	☹	☹	☺	☹	☹	☺	☹	☹	☺	☹	
16	월	일	월	일	☺	☺	☹	☹	☺	☹	☹	☺	☹	☹	☺	☹	

My Comment에는 공부하고 나서 느낀 소감을 간단히 적어보세요.

중학부터 시작하는 수능 독해 첫걸음

바로 읽는 배경지식 독해

LEVEL 3

생각의 폭을 넓히는 **배경지식 Story**

#*Topic* Andy Warhol & Pop Art

빨간 통조림이 반복적으로 나열된 그림을 본 적이 있나요? 이런 object를 그린 그림이 무슨 예술 작품이냐고 생각할 수 있겠지만 이 그림은 팝 아트를 대표하는 successful한 예술가인 앤디 워홀의 작품이에요. 팝 아트는 누구나 일상생활에서 쉽게 접할 수 있는 대중적인 것에서 소재를 찾은 예술이에요.

앤디 워홀 「캠벨 스프 캔」

대량 생산되는 product로부터 마릴린 먼로와 같은 celebrity, 만화 캐릭터까지 친숙한 소재를 사용했어요. 일반 대중에게 예술에 대해 일일이 explain하지 않아도 누구나 작품을 쉽게 이해할 수 있도록 말이죠.

팝 아트가 appear했던 1950년대 미국에서는 작가의 감정을 자유롭게 나타내는 추상표현주의가 예술의 흐름을 주도하고 있었어요. 대표 작가인 잭슨 폴록(Jackson Pollock)의 작품을 보면 점과 선으로 되어 있어 무슨 내용인지 제대로 recognize하기 어려워요. 대중에게 예술은 접근하기 어려운 것이라는 생각이 들게 하죠. 하지만 팝 아트는 이런 편견을 과감히 깨트리고 순수 예술과 commercial 예술의 경계를 허물었어요. 자 이제 '팝 아트의 왕자'라 불리는 앤디 워홀의 작품 속으로 함께 들어가 볼까요?

잭슨 폴록 「제 19번」

본문 미리보기 QUIZ

1 앤디 워홀의 작품이 비싼 이유는 작품이 [☐ 이해하기 어렵기 / ☐ 이해하기 쉽기] 때문이다.   10쪽에서 확인

2 앤디 워홀은 [☐ 미국의 피츠버그에서 / ☐ 영국의 런던에서] 태어났다.   12쪽에서 확인

☐ 1	**achieve** [ətʃíːv]	동 이루다	목표를 이루다	_____ a goal
☐ 2	**advertising** [ǽdvərtàiziŋ]	명 광고	이미지 광고	image _____
☐ 3	**appear** [əpíər]	동 나타나다	갑자기 나타나다	_____ suddenly
☐ 4	**celebrity** [səlébrəti]	명 유명 인사	세계적인 유명 인사	an international _____
☐ 5	**commercial** [kəmə́ːrʃəl]	형 상업적인	상업 미술	_____ art
☐ 6	**difference** [dífərəns]	명 차이	문화적 차이	cultural _____
☐ 7	**elevate** [éləvèit]	동 올리다	다리를 올리다	_____ one's leg
☐ 8	**explain** [ikspléin]	동 설명하다	간단하게 설명하다	_____ briefly
☐ 9	**modern** [mάdərn]	형 현대의	현대 무용	_____ dance
☐ 10	**object** [άbdʒikt]	명 물건	금속으로 된 물건	a metallic _____
☐ 11	**original** [ərídʒənl]	형 원래의	원본 파일	_____ file
☐ 12	**photograph** [fóutəgræf]	명 사진	사진을 촬영하다	take a _____
☐ 13	**product** [prάdəkt]	명 제품	신제품	new _____
☐ 14	**recognize** [rékəgnàiz]	동 알아보다	형체를 알아보다	_____ the shape
☐ 15	**successful** [səksésfəl]	형 성공적인	사업에 성공한	_____ in business

어휘 자신만만 QUIZ

1 그 작품의 원래 가격은 비싸지 않았다.

The _____ price of the work was not expensive.

2 그는 곧 성공적인 삽화가가 되었다.

He soon became a _____ illustrator.

Orange Marilyn

● My Reading Time I Words 206 / 2분 15초

1회 ____분____초 2회 ____분____초

"Orange Marilyn" is a 20-by-16 inch silkscreen work by Andy Warhol. He made it after Marilyn Monroe died in 1962. This style of art starts with a photograph. The artist then adds colors to change
5　the feeling in the photo. Some people say that Warhol was making a comment about a famous person in this picture. He was saying that, in modern society, a famous person seems more like a product than a person.

　　Warhol made several silkscreens showing Marilyn Monroe. The one called
10　"Orange Marilyn" is the most famous. That's because its price went sky high. The original price of the work was not expensive. First, it was sold to Leo Castelli for $250. When "Orange Marilyn" appeared at auction in 1998, after Warhol had died, however, it was sold for $17.3 million. The price was over 10,000 times the amount that Castelli had paid.

15　　Through the years, Warhol's works have been sold for more money than Picasso's. Why is his art so expensive? One reason is that it is not hard to understand. "If you hang a work of Jackson Pollock, few of your friends may recognize it," says the director of the Andy Warhol Museum. "With Warhol, you don't have to explain anything."

Words

photograph 몡 사진　　add 통 더하다　　comment 몡 논평　　modern 혱 현대의　　society 몡 사회
product 몡 제품　　original 혱 원래의　　expensive 혱 비싼　　appear 통 나타나다　　million 혱 백만
reason 몡 이유　　understand 통 이해하다　　recognize 통 알아보다　　explain 통 설명하다

Title

1 첫 번째 단락의 제목으로 가장 알맞은 것은?

a. "Orange Marilyn" and a Lucky Man, Leo Castelli

b. The Most Expensive Work by Andy Warhol

c. How "Orange Marilyn" Came into Being

d. The Sales History of "Orange Marilyn"

Details

2 Orange Marilyn에 관한 설명 중 본문의 내용과 일치하지 <u>않는</u> 것은?

a. Its size is 20 inches by 16 inches.

b. It was first sold for 250 dollars.

c. It is a silkscreen work by Andy Warhol.

d. It was sold to Leo Castelli for 17.3 million dollars.

Details

3 앤디 워홀의 작품이 비싼 이유는?

→ It is partly because his art is _____ .

Summary

4 본문의 단어를 이용하여 요약을 완성하시오.

"Orange Marilyn" is a _____ work by Andy Warhol. It was first sold at the price of _____ dollars. "Orange Marilyn" was put up at _____ in 1998, and its price was _____ dollars. The price was over _____ more than the original price. Andy Warhol's works of art are easy to _____ and this feature has contributed to their popularity.

지식백과

앤디 워홀의 실크스크린 기법

공판화 기법 중 하나로 스텐실을 만든 후 그 위에 잉크 등을 찍어서 구멍이 뚫린 곳에만 그림이 찍히도록 하는 기법이다. 색의 수에 따라서 한 가지 색을 차례대로 반복하면 겹쳐져서 작품이 완성된다. 앤디 워홀의 작품인 캠벨 수프 깡통, 코카콜라 병, 지폐, 유명인의 초상 등이 모두 실크스크린 기법으로 제작되었다.

▶ 앤디 워홀의 재미있는 작품 이야기를 동영상으로 만나 보세요. ⏱ Time 4' 35"

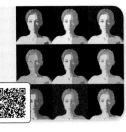

Reading 02

The Life of Andy Warhol

● My Reading Time ┃ Words 185 / 2분 03초

1회 _____ 분 _____ 초 2회 _____ 분 _____ 초

Andy Warhol was born in 1928 in Pittsburgh as a son of Slovak immigrants. He showed a talent for drawing and painting at an early age. He studied commercial art at the Carnegie Institute of Technology. After graduation, he went to New York and worked as an illustrator for magazines and commercial
5 advertising. He soon became a successful illustrator.

In the 1960s, Andy Warhol started painting daily objects such as Campbell Soup cans and Coke bottles. The idea of painting daily objects came from one of ⓐ his friends. ⓑ He suggested Andy should paint the things ⓒ he loved most. ⓓ Andy also loved celebrities, so he painted them as well. He made
10 silkscreen prints of famous people like Marilyn Monroe and Elizabeth Taylor. In 1962, he founded *The Factory*. He employed "art workers" and mass-produced his silkscreen prints with different versions.

Andy Warhol was called "the Prince of Pop
15 Art." He achieved this position through hard work. He was the artist who elevated subjects of everyday life to the level of art. He was also the one who removed the difference between fine art and commercial art.

Words

immigrant 명 이민자   commercial 형 상업적인   advertising 명 광고   successful 형 성공적인
illustrator 명 삽화가   object 명 물건   celebrity 명 유명 인사   found 동 설립하다   employ 동 고용하다
mass-produce 동 대량 생산하다   achieve 동 이루다   elevate 동 올리다   remove 동 제거하다

1 Topic

The first paragraph is mainly about _____.

a. Andy Warhol's family

b. Andy Warhol's early career

c. the world of Andy Warhol's works

d. Andy Warhol's position as a pop artist

2 Reference

Among ⓐ~ⓓ, which refers to a different person?

a. ⓐ   b. ⓑ   c. ⓒ   d. ⓓ

3 Details

Write T if the statement about Andy Warhol is true and F if it is false.

(1) _____ He loved Campbell Soup cans and Coke bottles.

(2) _____ He mass-produced his silkscreen prints.

(3) _____ He thought fine art was better than pop art.

4 Graphic Organizer

Complete the chart with the words from the passage.

Andy Warhol, the Prince of _____ _____

Birth	• born in _____ in 1928
Early career	• studied at the Carnegie Institute of Technology • became a successful _____ in New York
1960s	• started painting _____ objects and famous people • founded *The Factory* and mass-produced his _____ prints

지식백과

다재다능했던, 앤디 워홀

앤디 워홀은 미술가로서 뿐만 아니라 예술 분야 전반에 거쳐 다양한 활동을 펼쳤다. 1963년부터 1968년까지 수많은 영화를 만들어 영화 제작자로서 활동을 했고, 배우로 영화에 출현하기도 했다. 또한 <앤디 워홀의 15분>이라는 TV 프로그램을 만들었고, 작가로서 자서전, 회고록 등을 출간하였다.

The Prince of Pop Art · 13

Reading Closer

독해의 내공을 키우는 마무리 학습

A

Unit 01에서 학습한 단어를 생각해 보고, 다음 퍼즐을 완성해 보시오.

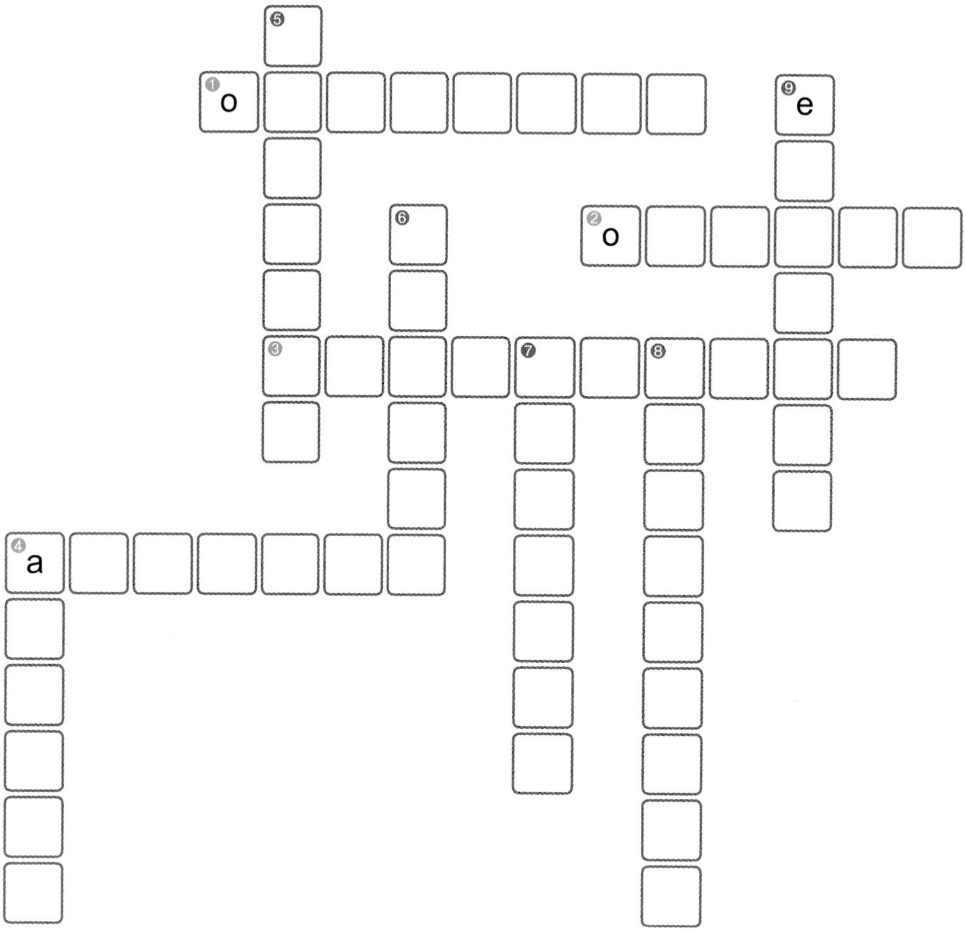

Across

❶ made or produced first

❷ 금속으로 된 물건: a metallic ________

❸ 상업 미술: ________ art

❹ to reach a goal

Down

❹ to begin to be seen

❺ 신제품: new ________

❻ ________ means move or take something away from a place.

❼ to make something clear or easy to understand

❽ A ________ is a person who is famous.

❾ to lift something up

B 다음 [보기]에서 알맞은 말을 골라 문장을 완성하시오.

| 보기 | commercial | expensive | elevate | recognize | achieve |

1 People did not _____ his talent when he was young.

2 The soccer player tried to _____ his goal by practicing hard.

3 The rent was so _____ that they had to move out.

4 Despite sharp criticism, the movie was a(n) _____ success.

5 Too much stress can _____ blood pressure levels.

🔅 생각을 키우는 서술형 · 수행평가 대비 훈련

C 다음 글을 읽고, 밑줄 친 부분 중 어색한 부분을 찾아 바르게 고치시오.

Pop art is an art ⓐ movement that started in the mid-1950s. This movement aimed to ⓑ remove the difference between fine art and commercial art, and Andy Warhol is one of the most famous artists who led the trend. He often chose ⓒ commercial images such as canned goods in his paintings. His works are ⓓ hard to understand, so they are very popular even among ordinary people who do not enjoy art. It is hard to believe that the total ⓔ value of his works is more than $496 million!

_____ → _____

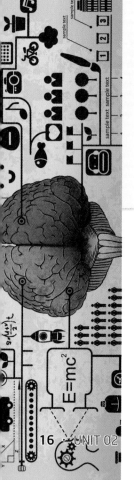

#*Topic* Brain, Memory & Information

망각하는 자에겐 복이 있다.

자신의 실수 또한 잊어버리기 때문이다.

〈프리드리히 니체〉

우리의 brain은 complex한 수많은 정보를 처리하고 기억해요. 시간이 지나면서 중요하지 않은 information은 점차 잊히기도 하고 중요한 것은 우리의 장기 기억에 survive해요. 하지만 과거의 memory가 하나도 빠짐없이 선명하게 머릿속에 last한다면 어떨까요?

실제로 세계적으로 몇 명 안 되는 이런 사람들이 존재한다니 정말 놀랍죠? 과거의 일을 정확히 기억하고 있는 증상을 과잉 기억 증후군(Hyperthymesia)이라고 해요. 미국의 질 프라이스라는 여성이 이 증후군을 앓고 있는데 자신의 물건을 잃어버린 적이 없을 정로도 기억력이 뛰어나다고 해요. 기억력이 좋으면 편리할 것 같지만 그녀는 forget하고 싶은 기억까지 계속 repeat되서 매우 고통스럽다고 고백했어요.

그녀의 놀라운 기억 능력을 검사해 본 결과 과거의 일들은 정확히 remember하는 반면 학습 영역에 해당하는 암기력이나 기타 인지 능력은 평범하다고 해요. 또한 일반 사람들은 과거의 기억을 뇌의 우전두엽에 저장하는 반면 과잉 기억 증후군을 앓고 있는 사람들은 우전두엽과 좌전두엽에 모두 저장한다고 밝혀졌어요. 아직도 우리 뇌의 활동 process는 풀리지 않은 의문들로 가득한데요. 이어지는 글에서 동물과 인간의 기억력에 관한 재미있는 이야기를 만나 보세요.

본문 미리보기 **QUIZ**

1 개는 어떤 일이 일어나면 [☐ 2분 후에 / ☐ 10분 후에] 그 사건을 잃어버릴 수 있다. 18쪽에서 확인

2 장기 기억력 향상에 도움이 되는 것은 [☐ 운동 / ☐ 수면] 이다. 20쪽에서 확인

□ 1	**allow** [əláu]	통 가능하게 하다	···을 가능하게 하다	_____ of something
□ 2	**brain** [brein]	명 뇌	뇌 손상	_____ damage
□ 3	**complex** [kámpleks]	형 복잡한	복잡한 기계	_____ machinery
□ 4	**connect** [kənékt]	통 연결하다	두 개의 방을 연결하다	_____ the two rooms
□ 5	**enhance** [inhǽns]	통 향상시키다	가치를 높이다	_____ the value
□ 6	**establish** [istǽbliʃ]	통 확립하다	이론을 확립하다	_____ a theory
□ 7	**forget** [fərgét]	통 잊어버리다	완전히 잊다	_____ completely
□ 8	**information** [ìnfərméiʃən]	명 정보	정보를 검색하다	search _____
□ 9	**last** [læst]	통 지속하다	오래 지속되다	_____ long
□ 10	**memory** [méməri]	명 기억	기억력이 좋다	have a good _____
□ 11	**network** [nétwə̀ːrk]	명 연결망	사회 연결망	social _____
□ 12	**process** [práses]	명 과정	노화 과정	the aging _____
□ 13	**remember** [rimémbər]	통 기억하다	올바로 기억하다	_____ correctly
□ 14	**repeat** [ripíːt]	통 반복하다	실수를 반복하다	_____ mistakes
□ 15	**survive** [sərváiv]	통 살아남다	그 전쟁에서 살아남다	_____ the war

어휘 자신만만 QUIZ

1 그들은 생존하도록 도와주는 것을 기억한다.

They remember things which help them _____.

2 두뇌는 그 정보가 충분히 중요한지를 판단한다.

The brain decides whether the _____ is important enough.

Animals and Memory

There is a big difference between a person's memory and a dog's. When you meet an old friend, you remember where and when you last met. You may even remember what you were wearing. In other words, you remember an event. Recent research indicates that dogs and other animals cannot do this. In fact, it seems that many animals have terrible short-term memories. Dogs may forget an event two minutes after it happens! Many animals, from dolphins to bees, have memories which only last seconds.

"But wait," you might say. "What about the saying 'an elephant never forgets' and things like that? Don't some animals have long memories?" In some ways, yes. They remember things which help them _____. For instance, some birds remember where they left their food. Animals also connect memories to feelings. When your dog remembers you, it remembers you are a good person, but it does not remember when and where you last met.

This difference is important because remembering events allows people to create history. We can 'time travel' into the past. Can animals do this? We don't think so.

Words difference 몡 차이   memory 몡 기억   remember 툉 기억하다   event 몡 사건, 일   indicate 툉 나타내다
short-term 톙 단기의   forget 툉 잊어버리다   last 툉 지속하다   survive 툉 살아남다   connect 툉 연결하다
allow 툉 가능하게 하다   create 툉 창조하다   history 몡 역사   past 몡 과거

LINK 실력 향상 WORKBOOK p.6

Main Idea

1 글의 요지로 가장 알맞은 것은?

a. Animals' memories are bad and different from humans'.

b. Both humans and animals remember events.

c. Animals remember things that are related to their survival.

d. Similarities exist in memory between humans and dogs.

Inference

2 본문의 빈칸에 들어갈 말로 가장 알맞은 것은?

a. create

b. survive

c. adapt

d. produce

Details

3 다음 중 본문의 내용과 일치하는 것은?

a. Animals remember past events.

b. Animals remember when you last met.

c. Animals connect memories to feelings.

d. Animals remember events in time order.

Summary

4 본문의 단어를 이용하여 요약을 완성하시오.

Animals seem to have bad _____ memories. They often last only _____. Animals do remember things that are related to survival and link memories to _____. They do not remember individual _____. For this reason, animals cannot create _____.

개, 고양이 누가 더 똑똑할까?

지식백과

대뇌 피질은 대뇌의 가장 표면에 있는 주름진 바깥층으로 시각, 촉각 등의 정보를 결합시켜 의사 결정 및 문제 해결을 유도한다. 뉴런은 정보 처리의 기본 단위인데 대뇌 피질에 뉴런이 많다는 것은 그만큼 인지 능력이 뛰어나다는 사실을 의미한다. 개는 약 5억 3천만 개, 고양이는 약 2억 5천만 개의 뉴런이 있다고 한다. 개의 지능이 고양이보다 두 배 이상 높다는 것을 나타낸다. 인간은 약 160억 개, 오랑우탄이나 고릴라는 60~70억 개, 코끼리는 56억 개의 뉴런이 있다.

Reading
02
Do You Have a Good Memory?

Remembering information is one of the most complex processes of the human brain. There are three types of memory: sensory, short-term, and long-term. Sensory memory is an exact copy of what we see or hear. The brain decides whether the information is important enough. If the information is important, it is sent to short-term or long-term memory. If it is not, it is soon forgotten. Sensory memory lasts less than a second.

Short-term memory can hold 7, plus or minus 2, items. The duration of short-term memory is usually a few seconds. Without this kind of memory, we can't work on problems. In writing an essay, for example, we must be able to keep the last sentence in mind as we write the next.

Long-term memory is like a huge network of data. This stores all the things we have remembered. Information in short-term memory goes into long-term memory when it is repeated or connected with something we already know. Some people believe that sleep is important in establishing long-term memory. They say the process of turning short-term memory into long-term memory is enhanced during sleep.

Words

information 명 정보   complex 형 복잡한   process 명 과정   sensory 형 감각의   exact 형 정확한
duration 명 지속되는 기간   sentence 명 문장   huge 형 거대한   network 명 연결망   store 동 저장하다
repeat 동 반복하다   establish 동 확립하다   enhance 동 향상시키다

• Topic

1 This passage is mainly about _____ .

a. three types of human memory

b. how to improve human memory

c. the role of long-term memory

d. how different memories affect learning

• Details

2 Which is NOT true according to the passage?

a. Sensory memory works when we see or hear something.

b. Short-term memory lasts less than a second.

c. Information is stored in long-term memory when it is repeated.

d. All the things we have remembered are stored in long-term memory.

• Inference

3 According to the passage, which memory works in each situation?

(1) Tony remembers that he went to the beach two years ago.

→ _____

(2) Julia heard Mike's phone number and wrote it down.

→ _____

• Graphic Organizer

4 Complete the map with the words from the passage.

Process of Human Memory

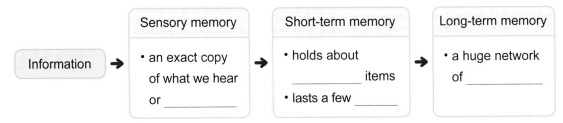

Sensory memory	Short-term memory	Long-term memory
• an exact copy of what we hear or _____	• holds about _____ items • lasts a few _____	• a huge network of _____

Information →

기억력 천재, 서번트 증후군

자폐증이나 지적 장애를 가진 사람이 암산, 기억, 음악 등 특정 분야에서 매우 우수한 능력을 발휘하는 현상이다. 서번트 증후군을 처음 발견한 사람은 다운 증후군을 발견했던 존 랭던 다운 박사이다. 1887년 일반 사람들보다 인지 및 대화 능력이 떨어지지만 특정 분야에서 뛰어난 능력을 보이는 사람들의 사례를 최초로 보고했다. 이 증후군을 가진 사람들은 좌뇌의 손상으로 우뇌의 기능이 탁월해져서 발생한다고 한다.

지식백과

○ 서번트 증후군으로 특별한 능력을 가진 사람들을 동영상으로 만나 보세요. ● Time 3' 58"

A Unit 02에서 학습한 단어를 생각해 보고, 다음 퍼즐을 완성해 보시오.

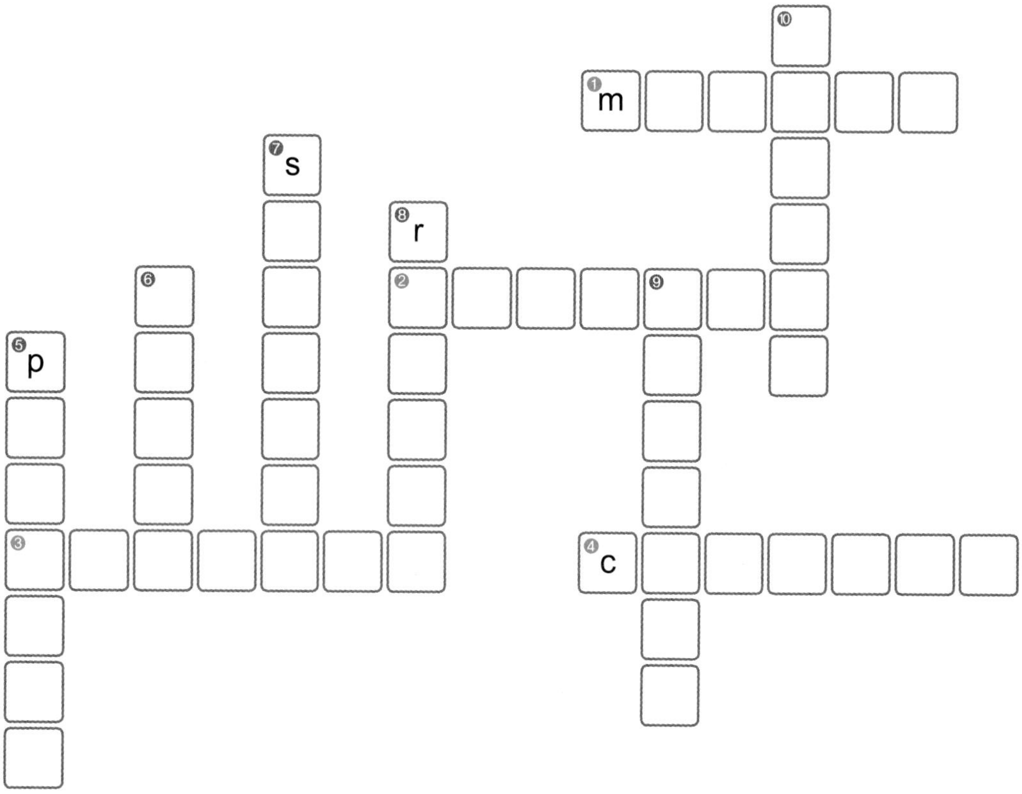

👉 **Across**

① 뛰어난 기억력: excellent _____

② a similar word of improve

③ _____ means join two or more things together.

④ not easy to understand or explain

👂 **Down**

⑤ 노화 과정: the aging _____

⑥ 뇌 손상: _____ damage

⑦ to remain alive, to continue to live

⑧ to say something again

⑨ 사회 연결망: social _____

⑩ to be unable to think of or remember something

B 다음 [보기]에서 알맞은 말을 골라 문장을 완성하시오.

보기	complex	connect	instance	duration	enhance

1 In this factory alone, for _____, 100 jobs were created.

2 Reading is a habit that will _____ your creativity.

3 The issues are _____, so we cannot solve them in a day.

4 Phones should be turned off for the _____ of the concert.

5 Please _____ the printer to the computer before you turn the printer on.

🔆 생각을 키우는 서술형 · 수행평가 대비 훈련

C 다음 [보기]에서 알맞은 말을 골라 글을 완성하시오.

I have a bad memory. My mom sometimes tells me to clean my room. But I soon forget. I told her, "I'm sorry. I think I have a terrible _____." She laughed and said, "Your brain decides if _____ is important. If it is not, you forget it. In other words, my words are not important to you." The next time she told me, I tried not to _____ her words. When I showed her my room, she was very excited. "You _____ed!" she said. "Now put this event in your _____ memory."

보기	remember	long-term	information	memory	forget

생각의 폭을 넓히는 **배경지식 Story**

#Topic Machu Picchu & Tourists

남아메리카에 위치한 페루는 역사적으로 찬란한 잉카 문명을 꽃피운 나라로 유명하죠. ancient 잉카인들은 돌로 종이 한 장 들어갈 틈이 없을 정도로 이음새가 완벽하고 enormous 한 건축물을 쌓아 올릴 정도로 고도의 문명을 이루었어요. 이러한 건물들은 중앙아메리카를 여러 번 강타한 지진에서도 살아남았으니 정말 놀랍고 mysterious하지 않을 수가 없어요. 이렇게 지진도 이겨낸 잉카의 건물들을 누가 폐허로 만든 걸까요? 바로 스페인의 침략자들이에요. 이 위대한 civilization도 프란시스코 피사로와 스페인 침략자들 앞에서는 속수무책으로 무너져 내렸어요. 그들은 수많은 원주민을 죽이고 신전을 destroy하고 자신들의 건물을 세웠어요. 하지만 곳곳에 remain한 돌담과 돌길에 서린 잉카인들의 지혜와 솜씨마저 앗아갈 수는 없었어요.

오늘날 전 세계의 수많은 tourist들이 historic한 잉카 문명의 유적지를 보려고 페루를 방문해요. 특히 공중 도시라고 불리는 마추픽추에는 많은 인파가 몰려들고 있어요. 하지만 많은 방문객들로 인해 고대 유적지가 damage되는 것은 아닌지 걱정하는 사람들이 많아요. 마추픽추에 관한 글을 읽으며 이 문제에 대해 좀 더 생각해 보도록 해요.

〈쿠스코의 돌담길〉

본문 미리보기 QUIZ

1 Adelmo는 마추픽추 관광객을 [☐ 더 끌어들여야 / ☐ 제한해야] 한다고 생각한다. 26쪽에서 확인

2 마추픽추는 [☐ 히말라야 산맥 / ☐ 안데스 산맥] 에 있는 고대 도시이다. 28쪽에서 확인

☐ 1	**ancient** [éinʃənt]	형 고대의	고대에는	in _____ times
☐ 2	**blade** [bleid]	명 (칼, 도구 등의) 날	면도날	a razor _____
☐ 3	**civilization** [sìvəlizéiʃən]	명 문명	동양 문명	oriental _____
☐ 4	**culture** [kʌ́ltʃər]	명 문화	문화 충격	_____ shock
☐ 5	**damage** [dǽmidʒ]	명 손상	손해를 입히다	cause _____
☐ 6	**destroy** [distrɔ́i]	통 파괴하다	자연을 파괴하다	_____ nature
☐ 7	**economy** [ikánəmi]	명 경제	세계 경제	the world _____
☐ 8	**endanger** [indéindʒər]	통 위험에 빠뜨리다	목숨을 위태롭게 하다	_____ one's life
☐ 9	**enormous** [inɔ́ːrməs]	형 거대한	엄청난 재산	_____ wealth
☐ 10	**environment** [inváiərənmənt]	명 환경	환경 친화적인	_____-friendly
☐ 11	**historic** [histɔ́(ː)rik]	형 역사적인	역사적 순간	a _____ moment
☐ 12	**mysterious** [mistíəriəs]	형 신비한	불가사의한 사건	a _____ event
☐ 13	**remain** [riméin]	통 남아있다	아름답게 남아있다	_____ beautiful
☐ 14	**structure** [strʌ́ktʃər]	명 건축물	석조 건축물	a stone _____
☐ 15	**tourist** [túərist]	명 관광객	관광 명소	_____ attraction

어휘 자신만만 QUIZ

1 관광객이 너무 많으면 고대 유물에 좋지 않을지도 모릅니다.

Too many _____ may not be good for the old ruins.

2 이곳은 세계에서 가장 아름답고 신비로운 장소들 중의 하나이다.

It is one of the most beautiful and _____ places in the world.

Reading 01

More Visitors to Machu Picchu?

REPORTER: Some people in Peru want more and more tourists to visit Machu Picchu. But others say it is not a good idea. What do you think about having more visitors to the historic site?

ADELMO: I live near Machu Picchu. Peru should try harder to bring more
5 tourists here. They will spend money here and make the local economy strong. There will be more jobs for us. Also, international tourists and the local people can learn about each other's cultures. Finally, people will realize that taking good care of Machu Picchu is important. So, it will remain beautiful for a long time.

10 **BEATRIZ:** I think Peru should limit the number of tourists who can visit Machu Picchu every year. There are too many tourists already, and it creates some serious problems. First, too many tourists may not be good for the old ruins. Visitors can damage the ruins little by little. Some of them may even move or break some of the ancient stones. Second, some tourists harm the environment.
15 They leave trash everywhere. If more people visit Machu Picchu, it can easily turn into an ugly place.

Words

tourist 명 관광객   historic 형 역사적인   site 명 장소   local 형 지역의   economy 명 경제
international 형 국제적인   culture 명 문화   realize 통 깨닫다   remain 통 남아있다   limit 통 제한하다
ruins 명 유적   damage 명 손상   ancient 형 고대의   harm 통 손상시키다   environment 명 환경

Topic

1 다음 문장의 빈칸에 가장 알맞은 것은?

> Adelmo and Beatriz give _____ answers to the reporter's question.

a. similar   b. different   c. unclear   d. the same

Inference

2 다음 중 Adelmo가 동의할 것 같은 문장은?

a. Machu Picchu should be open to local people only.

b. More people should come and see Machu Picchu.

c. Peru should not spend any money on Machu Picchu.

d. The ancient stones should be moved away.

Details

3 문장을 읽고, Adelmo의 의견에 A, Beatriz의 의견에 B를 쓰시오.

(1) _____ More visitors mean more business in the area.

(2) _____ Some visitors ruin the historic site.

(3) _____ Machu Picchu won't remain beautiful for long because of tourists.

Graphic Organizer

4 본문의 단어를 이용하여 표를 완성하시오.

Should we have more visitors to Machu Picchu?

Pros-Adelmo	Cons-Beatriz
① The local _____ will get stronger. ② There will be chances to learn about other _____. ③ People will realize it is _____ to take care of the site.	① Visitors can damage the ruins. ② Visitors can harm the _____.

공정 여행이란?

많은 사람들은 가이드를 따라 유명한 관광지를 둘러본 후, 대형 쇼핑센터나 호텔에서 시간을 보내는 것을 '여행'이라고 생각할 것이다. 최근 이런 여행이 지역 사회에 미치는 부정적인 영향을 지적하면서 새로운 형태의 여행을 제시하는 사람들이 늘고 있다. 현지의 환경에 해를 끼치지 않으면서 그 지역 사회에 도움을 주고자 하는 여행을 '공정 여행'이라고 한다. 현지인이 운영하는 숙소와 음식점 이용하기, 멸종 위기에 놓인 동식물로 만든 기념품 사지 않기, 현지의 생활 방식을 존중하기 등의 공정 여행 방법이 있다.

▶ 공정 여행의 의미를 동영상으로 만나 보세요. ● Time 4' 56"

An Ancient City of Mysteries

Machu Picchu is an ancient city in the Andes Mountains. It was built around 1450. It is one of the most beautiful and mysterious places in the world. When the Inca civilization was destroyed by the Spanish, the city

5 was forgotten. It became known to the outside world when an American historian, Hiram Bingham, found it in 1911.

There are hundreds of stone structures in the city. It has palaces, temples,

10 parks, fountains, and houses. Many buildings were built without mortar. Blocks of stone were cut to fit together perfectly. Some people say that they are so perfect that even the blade of a knife can't be put between the stones. Many of the building blocks weigh 50 tons or more. (A) How they moved and placed enormous blocks of stone remains a mystery. They had no horses or wheels! (B)

15 People from all over the world come to see Machu Picchu. (C) Now it is on the list of 100 Most Endangered Sites. (D)

Words

mysterious 형 신비한   civilization 명 문명   destroy 동 파괴하다   outside 형 외부의   historian 명 역사가   structure 명 건축물   fountain 명 분수   mortar 명 모르타르, 회반죽   blade 명 (칼 등의) 날   weigh 동 ~의 무게가 나가다   enormous 형 거대한   endanger 동 위험에 처하다

Topic

1

This passage is mainly about _____.

a. the location of Machu Picchu

b. precious stones of Machu Picchu

c. the history and some wonders of Machu Picchu

d. endangered places in the world

Details

2

Write T if the statement is true and F if it is false.

(1) _____ Hiram Bingham discovered Machu Picchu in 1450.

(2) _____ The stone structures in Machu Picchu weren't built with mortar.

(3) _____ Horses were used to move heavy blocks of stone.

Organization

3

Where would the following sentence best fit?

> As more tourists visit Machu Picchu, however, there is a growing danger.

a. (A)   b. (B)   c. (C)   d. (D)

Summary

4

Complete the summary with the words from the passage.

> Machu Picchu is a very old city. It was _____ in the 15th century, destroyed
> by the _____, and discovered by Hiram Bingham in _____. People
> built _____ structures there without mortar. They moved and placed
> many blocks of stone in a mysterious way. Sadly, the city is in danger
> because of the increasing number of _____.

지식 백과

쿠스코의 '12각 돌'

고대 잉카인들은 돌의 모양을 완벽하게 끼워 맞춰 모르타르 없이 석조 건축물을 쌓아 올렸다고 한다. 잉카 문명의 놀라운 건축술을 잘 알려 주는 예로 쿠스코의 아르마스 광장에 12각 돌이 있다. 이 12각 돌에는 12 달을 상징하는 12개의 면이 있고 이 면이 모두 들어맞도록 돌을 끼워 넣었다. 잉카인들은 철기를 사용하지 도 않고 돌이나 청동 칼을 사용하여 지었다고 한다.

A Unit 03에서 학습한 단어를 생각해 보고, 다음 퍼즐을 완성해 보시오.

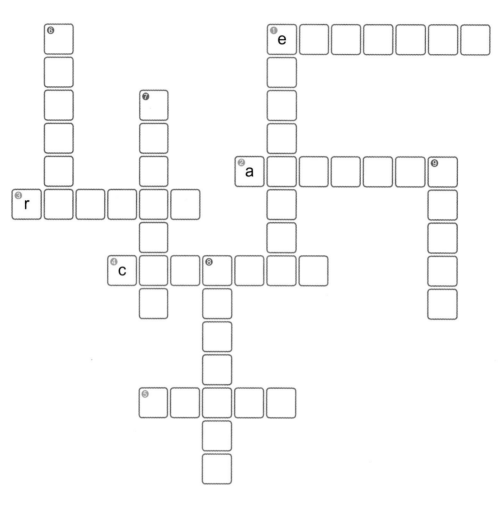

☞ Across

❶ 세계 경제: the world _____

❷ belonging to a time that was long ago in the past

❸ 아름답게 남아있다: _____ beautiful

❹ 문화 충격: _____ shock

❺ to find how heavy someone or something is

Down

❶ to cause someone or something to be in a dangerous place or situation

❻ the opposite of benefit

❼ 심각한 얼굴: a _____ look

❽ A _____ is a person who travels to a place for pleasure.

❾ a similar word of garbage

B 다음 [보기]에서 알맞은 말을 골라 문장을 완성하시오.

보기	endanger	tourist	ancient	mystery	ruins

1 The modern building is one of the city's most popular _____ attractions.

2 World Wildlife Fund tries hard to protect _____ed animals.

3 There are _____ of Baekje Dynasty in Gong-Ju.

4 How they carried the heavy rock is still a _____.

5 It was _____ Egyptians who invented such things as pens, locks and keys, and toothpaste.

🔅 **생각을 키우는 서술형 · 수행평가 대비 훈련**

C 다음 [보기]에서 알맞은 말을 골라 글을 완성하시오.

Hello, I'm Kastro. I was born in Cusco and have lived here for long time. We are happy that a lot of _____ visit Cusco to see our _____ attractions. One of the most beautiful and _____ attractions is Machu Picchu. There are hundreds of structures made of _____ which fit together perfectly. It seems that it is a mystery how our ancestors _____ the stone structures on the top of the mountain without vehicles. Before you visit, remember this. It is our responsibility to protect our amazing historic sites for the next generation.

보기	tourists	stones	historic	mysterious	built

#*Topic* Volcanos, Etna & Harmony

과학적인 지식이 부족했던 옛날에는 어떤 자연 현상이 왜 일어나는 것인지 모르는 경우가 많았어요. 그중에 뜨거운 불과 ash를 뿜어내고 소리가 요란한 active 화산의 경우는 어떻게 느꼈을까요? 고대 그리스 로마 시대의 사람들은 산이 erupt하는 것을 불의 신 헤파이스토스가 작업 중인 신호라고 생각했어요. 수천 년간 불을 뿜어 온 시칠리아 섬의 에트나 화산 underground에 헤파이스토스 대장간이 있어서 solid한 쇠를 힘껏 때릴 때마다 에트나 화산이 폭발음과 함께 불꽃이 튀어나왔다고 말이죠. 참 재미있는 생각이죠?

Volcano는 땅속에 melt되어 있는 마그마가 지각의 틈을 통해 땅 위로 뿜어져 나오면서 만들어진 산이에요. 우리 가까운 곳에도 화산 작용으로 이루어진 산과 섬이 있는데요. 백두산, 한라산, 울릉도가 바로 화산 활동으로 만들어졌다고 해요. 제주도와 울릉도는 바다 밑에서 화산이 폭발해서 이루어진 화산섬이에요. 현재는 모두 standstill한 상태이지만 1만 년 내에 분출한 적이 있는 화산은 alive한 화산으로 분류하기 때문에 이 세 곳 모두가 현재 활화산이랍니다. 가장 폭발 가능성이 높은 화산은 백두산인데요. 2000년도 초반에 화산 지진이 3,000회 이상 발생하는 등 재분화의 조짐이 엿보인다고 해요. 따라서 언제, 어떤 규모로 폭발할지 지속적인 연구가 필요하죠.

본문 미리보기 QUIZ

1 에트나산은 [☐ 유럽에서 가장 높은 휴화산] 이다.
　　　　　　[☐ 유럽에서 가장 높은 활화산]

34쪽에서 확인

2 지구는 [☐ 중심핵, 맨틀, 지각] 으로 이루어져 있다.
　　　　　[☐ 맨틀, 지각]

36쪽에서 확인

☐ 1	**active** [金ktiv]	형 활동적인	활화산	_____ volcano
☐ 2	**alive** [əláiv]	형 살아있는	싱싱해 보이다	look _____
☐ 3	**ash** [æʃ]	명 재	담뱃재	cigarette _____
☐ 4	**circumstance** [sə́:rkəmstæns]	명 상황	사회적 환경	social _____
☐ 5	**consider** [kənsídər]	통 고려하다	제안을 고려하다	_____ a suggestion
☐ 6	**core** [kɔːr]	명 중심부	대도시 중심부	_____ city
☐ 7	**crater** [kréitər]	명 분화구	달 분화구	moon _____
☐ 8	**erupt** [irʌ́pt]	통 분출하다	갑자기 분출하다	_____ suddenly
☐ 9	**harmony** [háːrməni]	명 조화	조화롭게 살다	live in _____
☐ 10	**material** [mətíəriəl]	명 물질, 재료	유독성 물질	toxic _____
☐ 11	**melt** [melt]	통 녹다	불에 녹다	_____ in a fire
☐ 12	**solid** [sálid]	형 단단한	단단한 땅	_____ ground
☐ 13	**standstill** [stǽndstìl]	명 멈춤	정지하다	come to a _____
☐ 14	**underground** [ʌ̀ndərgráund]	형 지하의	지하 차고	an _____ garage
☐ 15	**volcano** [vɑlkéinou]	명 화산	휴화산	silent _____

어휘 자신만만 QUIZ

1 아마도 그들은 에트나산과 조화롭게 살아가는 법을 알고 있는지도 모른다.

Perhaps they know how to live in _____ with Mount Etna.

2 뜨거운 가스, 화산재, 그리고 용암 때문에 화산은 강력하고 위험할 수 있다.

A _____ can be powerful and dangerous because of the hot gas, ash, and lava.

Reading 01

Living with Etna

Mount Etna, which is more than 3,327 meters high, is Europe's highest active volcano. The loud noise, smoke, and gas that come from the mountain remind people that Etna is alive. It could erupt at anytime.

Despite the dangers of this active volcano, many people have had a strong
5   bond with Mount Etna. For centuries, people have lived near the mountain, which sits on the eastern coast of Sicily, Italy. Today, thousands of people still live there and farm the land. Volcanic ash makes the soil rich and good for farming, so they grow various crops there. Also, these people make money from the large number of tourists who come to see the volcano firsthand. It is
10   no wonder that Mount Etna was declared a UNESCO World Heritage in 2013.

(A) Mount Etna is a great place to visit but not an easy place to live. (B) The town of Nicolasi, just 19 kilometers from the crater, has been destroyed twice. The villages near the crater face danger every day. (C) However, the people have not moved away. (D)

Words   active 휑 활동적인   volcano 몡 화산   remind 동 상기시키다   alive 휑 살아있는   erupt 동 분출하다
despite 젼 …에도 불구하고   bond 몡 유대   century 몡 백 년   ash 몡 재   soil 몡 토양   various 휑 다양한
crop 몡 농작물   firsthand 뷔 직접   declare 동 선언하다   crater 몡 분화구   harmony 몡 조화

Topic

1 본문의 요지로 가장 알맞은 것은?

a. Volcanoes are highly active and dangerous.

b. People face danger but live near a volcano.

c. Tourists love to visit dangerous volcanoes.

d. The small villages of Italy are loved by tourists.

Organization

2 주어진 문장이 들어가기에 가장 알맞은 곳은?

> Perhaps they know how to live in harmony with Mount Etna.

a. (A)   b. (B)   c. (C)   d. (D)

Details

3 다음 중 본문의 내용과 일치하지 <u>않는</u> 것은?

a. Mount Etna is an active volcano.

b. Farming is possible near the volcano.

c. Visitors help people who live near the volcano earn money.

d. The town of Nicolasi has always been a safe place to live.

Summary

4 본문의 단어를 이용하여 요약을 완성하시오.

> Mount Etna in Italy is the highest _____ volcano in Europe. Although it is dangerous, people still live near it. Because of volcanic _____, the land has _____ soil. Also, lots of tourists bring _____ into the local economy. Despite the dangers near the crater, people keep living there.

지식백과

세상에서 제일 큰 화산 - 마우나로아산

미국 하와이에 있는 마우나로아(Mauna Loa)산은 높이 약 4,100미터로 세계에서 가장 큰 화산이다. 하와이 섬을 이루는 다섯 개 화산 중 하나로 활화산이다. 1832년 이후 45회 이상의 분출이 있었고, 1950년에 용암 20톤을 방출하는 마지막 대분화가 있었다. 국립공원으로 지정되어 많은 관광객들이 찾고 있다.

How Volcanoes Erupt

● My Reading Time l Words 194 / 2분 05초

1회 ____분 ____초 **2회** ____분 ____초

To understand how a volcano works, we need to consider the structure of the planet. The Earth has three layers: the core, the mantle, and the outer crust. The core is at the center of the Earth and consists of solid rock. People live on the solid outer crust, (A) that / which is about 5 to 50 kilometers
5   thick. The largest layer, called the mantle, is between the core and the outer crust. For the most part, it stays (B) solid / solidly .

In certain circumstances, the mantle material melts. It forms hot liquid rock called magma. Magma gathers in a large underground pool. When the pressure gets strong enough, a weak spot in the outer crust cracks, and the
10   magma shoots up in the form of lava.

A volcano can be powerful and dangerous because of the hot gas, ash, and lava. For example, the Eyjafjallajökull [Ay-ya-fyala-yo-cul] volcano in Iceland erupted in 2010. Ash clouds covered much of Europe. Tens of thousands of tourists had to wait for days to get home because planes stopped flying. The
15   flow of lava and ash also destroyed many farms near the volcano. The eruption brought a lot of human activities to a standstill.

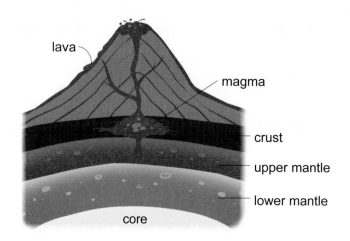

Words

consider 통 고려하다   planet 명 행성   layer 명 층   core 명 중심부   mantle 명 맨틀   crust 명 지각
consist of …로 구성하다   solid 형 단단한   circumstance 명 상황   material 명 재료   melt 통 녹다
underground 형 지하의   crack 명 갈라진 금   standstill 명 멈춤

1 • Title

Another title for the passage could be " _____."

a. The Structure of the Planet

b. Where Does Lava Come From?

c. Volcanoes: Formation and Power

d. The Most Dangerous Volcano in the World

2 • Details

Write T if the statement is true and F if it is false.

(1) _____ The core of the planet is partly hot liquid.

(2) _____ Lava remains inside the outer crust of the Earth.

(3) _____ The volcano in Iceland caused a lot of trouble.

3 • Grammar

Choose the words that fit in boxes (A) and (B).

	(A)	(B)		(A)	(B)
a.	that	⋯⋯ solid	b.	which	⋯⋯ solid
c.	that	⋯⋯ solidly	d.	which	⋯⋯ solidly

4 • Graphic Organizer

Complete the map with the words from the passage.

How Volcanoes Erupt

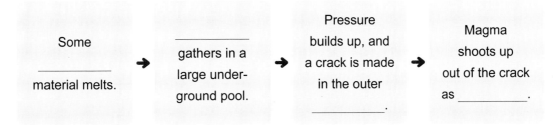

Some _____ material melts. ➡ _____ gathers in a large underground pool. ➡ Pressure builds up, and a crack is made in the outer _____. ➡ Magma shoots up out of the crack as _____.

지식백과

환태평양 조산대

태평양을 둘러싸고 있는 조산대로, 뉴질랜드에서부터 동남아, 일본, 알류샨 열도, 북아메리카 록키산맥, 남아메리카 안데스산맥까지 이르는 약 40,000km 길이에 달한다. 지구상의 지진 중 약 90%가 이 '불의 고리'를 따라 발생하고, 활화산 중 약 75%가 이 곳에 분포한다.

◉ 화산 폭발의 원리는 동영상으로 확인해 보세요. ● Time 2' 17"

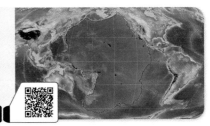

A Unit 04에서 학습한 단어를 생각해 보고, 다음 퍼즐을 완성해 보시오.

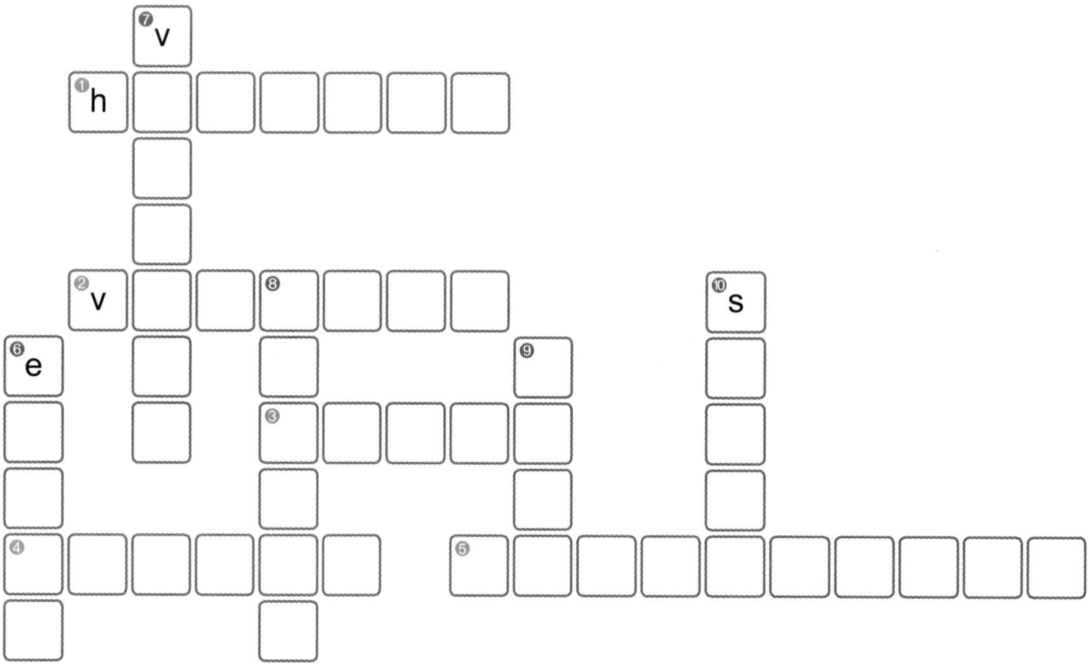

Across

❶ 조화롭게 살다: live in _____

❷ 화산재: _____ ash

❸ the opposite of dead

❹ 외행성: outer _____

❺ A _____ is a state in which all activity or motion is stopped.

Down

❻ to send out rocks, ash, lava

❼ 다양한 장소: _____ places

❽ 달 분화구: moon _____

❾ to change from a solid to a liquid usually because of heat

❿ a similar word of firm or hard

B 다음 [보기]에서 알맞은 말을 골라 문장을 완성하시오.

보기	core	solid	erupt	soil	standstill

1 What happens when volcanoes _____ underwater?

2 The Earth's _____ is in the middle of the Earth.

3 You should have rich _____ to grow hot peppers indoors.

4 My dad did not eat _____ food for several days.

5 Everything is at a _____ and many people have nowhere to go.

🔅 생각을 키우는 서술형·수행평가 대비 훈련

C 다음 [보기]에서 알맞은 말을 골라 글을 완성하시오.

Maria lives near Mount Etna. She has heard stories about the _____ all her life. If the volcano erupts, it can send hot gas, ash, and lava into the air. The ash clouds can _____ problems if planes have to stop flying. However, the volcanic _____ is also good for the soil. That is why Maria's family, as well as her neighbors, have lived in this area for a hundred years. They are _____. However, Maria is not sure she will be a farmer forever. Maybe she will work with tourists instead. She will show them the volcano _____.

보기	cause	firsthand	farmers	ash	volcano

UNIT **05** Coffee, Please!

#Topic Coffee, Italian-style & Fair Trade

커피를 좋아하는 것으로 유명한 나라하면 터키가 있어요. 터키의 커피 문화는 유네스코 무형 유산에 등재되어 있다고 해요. 터키 속담에 "커피 한 잔을 마시면 40년 동안 기억한 다."라는 말이 있어요. 함께 커피를 마신 사람과 40년간 인연 을 지속한다는 의미인데요. 그들의 society에서 커피가 얼마 나 중요한 문화인지를 보여 주는 것 같아요. 여러분은 coffee 하면 무엇이 떠오르나요? 안락한 atmosphere, 좋은 음악, 반가운 사람과 나누는 이야기 등을 떠올릴 거예요.

하지만 어떤 사람들은 커피 뒤에 숨은 농부들의 눈물을 생각했어요. 대규모 커피 회사들이 fair한 가격이 아닌 매우 낮은 가격으로 커피를 구매해서 소규모의 커피 농부들은 profit이 낮 아 재배 cost 조차도 감당을 못한다고 해요.

공정 무역은 이렇게 어려움에 처한 농가를 돕기 위해 시작된 movement예요. 공정 무역 인 증을 받은 agricultural product는 '공정한' 절차를 거쳐 trade되었다는 것을 나타내요. 이 제 농부들의 삶이 더 나아지기를 원하는 consumer들이라면, 공정 무역 마크가 있는 물건을 구매해서 이들을 도울 수 있어요! 자신의 소비 행동에 responsibility를 지는 멋진 일에 우리 모두 동참해 보는 것은 어떨까요?

본문 미리보기 QUIZ

1 하워드 슐츠는 [☐ 이탈리아 / ☐ 그리스의] 의 커피 문화를 미국에 가져왔다. 42쪽에서 확인

2 공정 무역 운동은 [☐ 생산자들 / ☐ 판매자들] 의 이익을 보호하기 위한 운동이다. 44쪽에서 확인

☐ 1 **agricultural** [æ̀grikʌ́ltʃərəl] 형 농업의 　　농산물 　　＿＿＿＿＿＿ product

☐ 2 **atmosphere** [ǽtməsfiər] 명 분위기 　　친근한 분위기 　　friendly ＿＿＿＿＿＿

☐ 3 **consumer** [kənsjúːmər] 명 소비자 　　소비자 권리 　　＿＿＿＿＿＿ rights

☐ 4 **cost** [kɔ(:)st] 명 비용 　　높은 주거 비용 　　high ＿＿＿＿ of housing

☐ 5 **create** [kriéit] 동 창조하다 　　일자리를 만들다 　　＿＿＿＿＿＿ jobs

☐ 6 **education** [èdʒukéiʃən] 명 교육 　　특수 교육 　　special ＿＿＿＿＿＿

☐ 7 **fair** [fɛər] 형 공정한 　　공정한 결정 　　＿＿＿＿＿＿ decision

☐ 8 **force** [fɔːrs] 동 강요하다 　　문을 억지로 열다 　　＿＿＿＿＿＿ a door open

☐ 9 **movement** [múːvmənt] 명 움직임 　　평화 운동 　　peace ＿＿＿＿＿＿

☐ 10 **product** [prádʌkt] 명 제품 　　제품을 개발하다 　　develop a ＿＿＿＿＿＿

☐ 11 **profit** [práfit] 명 이윤 　　이윤 배분 　　＿＿＿＿＿＿ sharing

☐ 12 **responsibility** [rispànsəbíləti] 명 책임 　　책임을 지다 　　take ＿＿＿＿＿＿ for

☐ 13 **society** [səsáiəti] 명 사회 　　다문화 사회 　　a multicultural ＿＿＿＿＿＿

☐ 14 **technical** [téknikəl] 형 기술적인 　　기술 지원 　　＿＿＿＿＿＿ support

☐ 15 **trade** [treid] 명 거래, 무역 　　자유 무역 　　free ＿＿＿＿＿＿

어휘 자신만만 QUIZ

1 스타벅스는 이제 사회에서의 역할에 대한 책임을 지려고 한다.

Starbucks now tries to take ＿＿＿＿＿＿＿＿ for its role in society.

2 커피는 세상에서 가장 많이 거래되는 농산물 중에 하나이다.

Coffee is one of the most traded ＿＿＿＿＿＿＿＿ products in the world.

An Italian-style Coffee Shop

🕐 My Reading Time | Words 186 / 2분

1회 ____분____초 2회 ____분____초

Now Starbucks is the largest coffee shop company in the world, with more than 28,000 stores in 76 countries. When it opened in 1971, however, it was just a small shop in downtown Seattle.

In 1981, Howard Schultz walked into a coffee bean store called Starbucks.
5 He was impressed with Starbucks' coffee and its business, and joined a year later. In 1983, he went on a trip to Italy. To his surprise, the Italian coffee bars were wonderful places for meeting people. He had a vision to bring the Italian tradition back to the United States.

When Howard became CEO of Starbucks, he put his vision into action. He
10 created a comfortable atmosphere in all his shops. Starbucks became a place to meet friends, take a rest, read books, enjoy music, and even study or work. People liked it, and Starbucks became popular quickly both at home and abroad.

Starbucks now tries to take responsibility for its role in society. It uses recycled paper cups. It also pays attention to the fair trade movement. It makes
15 sure that more items on its menu are fair trade products.

Words company 몡 회사   be impressed with …에 감명을 받다   vision 몡 꿈, 전망   tradition 몡 전통   create 통 창조하다   comfortable 혱 편안한   atmosphere 몡 분위기   responsibility 몡 책임   society 몡 사회   pay attention to …에 주목하다   fair 혱 공정한   trade 몡 거래   movement 몡 움직임   product 몡 제품

1 • Title

본문의 다른 제목으로 가장 알맞은 것은?

a. Starbucks Goes to Italy

b. Starbucks' Past and Present

c. The Most Expensive Coffee in the World

d. People Who Love the CEO of Starbucks

2 • Inference

밑줄 친 **his vision**의 의미로 알맞은 것은?

a. Coffee should be good and cheap.

b. Coffee should be imported from Italy.

c. A coffee shop should join the fair trade movement.

d. A coffee shop should be a comfortable place.

3 • Details

문장을 읽고 본문의 내용과 일치하면 T, 일치하지 않으면 F를 쓰시오.

(1) _____ Starbucks can be found in 76 countries.

(2) _____ Howard Schultz started to work for Starbucks in 1983.

(3) _____ Starbucks is concerned about the environment and fair trade.

4 • Graphic Organizer

본문의 단어를 이용하여 Starbucks에 대한 표를 완성하시오.

The History of Starbucks

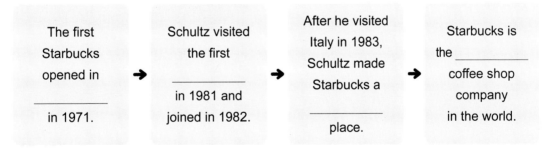

The first Starbucks opened in _____ in 1971. → Schultz visited the first _____ in 1981 and joined in 1982. → After he visited Italy in 1983, Schultz made Starbucks a _____ place. → Starbucks is the _____ coffee shop company in the world.

지식백과

커피의 가공 방식

커피나무가 자라 열매를 맺고 그 열매가 빨갛게 익으면 수확을 한다. 수확한 커피는 껍질과 과육을 벗겨낸 후 물에 씻어 말리거나 과육이 그대로 붙어 있는 채로 자연 건조하기도 한다. 이후 고온에서 볶는 과정을 거쳐 구수한 향이 나는 커피가 된다.

● 커피의 수확 과정을 동영상으로 확인해 보세요. ● Time 2' 22''

Fair Trade Coffee

Coffee is one of the most traded agricultural products in the world. But few people know that many small coffee growers can't even cover the costs of production. Coffee prices in the world market have fallen because large coffee companies force farmers to sell coffee at a (A) ⏤low / high⏤ price.

5　The fair trade movement is a possible solution to this problem. The idea is that farmers should share in some of the profits. Organizations give a fair trade mark to a company that joins the movement. To get this mark, a company must pay the farmers at least $1.40 per pound. It must also lend money to farmers and give technical help for farming. _____,

10　more farmers are now better off and receive health care as well as education.

The fair trade movement has become a consumer trend. More and more people care about the conditions of coffee growers. Coffee lovers are happy because they know this fact:

15　the more they drink coffee, the (B) ⏤better / worse⏤ the lives of the coffee growers get.

Words　agricultural 형 농업의　cover 동 돈을 대다　cost 명 비용　price 명 가격　force 동 강요하다　possible 형 가능한　solution 명 해결책　profit 명 이윤　organization 명 단체, 기구　technical 형 기술적인　better off 형편이 더 나은　education 명 교육　consumer 명 소비자　trend 명 추세　condition 명 상태

Main Idea

1 What is the main idea of the passage?

a. Fair trade coffee is healthier.

b. The coffee trade is becoming fairer to farmers.

c. Coffee prices have recently fallen sharply.

d. Coffee lovers welcome cheaper imported coffee.

Inference

2 Which one best fits in the blank?

a. Without such companies

b. Thanks to this movement

c. Because of large-scale farming

d. In addition to coffee lovers

Words

3 Choose the words that fit in boxes (A) and (B).

	(A)	(B)		(A)	(B)
a.	low	better	b.	low	worse
c.	high	better	d.	high	worse

Summary

4 Complete the summary with the words from the passage.

> Many small coffee growers used to be poor because of _____ coffee prices. The _____ trade movement is solving this problem. A coffee company can get a fair trade _____ by paying a good price, lending money to farmers, and giving _____ help. Because of this movement, farmers' conditions are getting better.

윤리적 소비란?

지식백과

생산자들에게 공정한 근로의 대가를 지불하는 공정 무역과 함께 시작된 소비자 운동으로, 노동자와 동물을 착취하여 만들어 낸 상품보다는 조금 더 비싸고 번거롭더라도 인간과 환경에 유익한 정당한 절차를 거친 상품을 구매하는 것을 말한다. 예를 들어, 소비자들이 상품의 질과 가격 뿐 아니라 그 상품이 사회나 환경에 미치는 영향까지 고려하여 구매를 결정하는 것이 윤리적 소비에 해당한다.

A Unit 05에서 학습한 단어를 생각해 보고, 다음 퍼즐을 완성해 보시오.

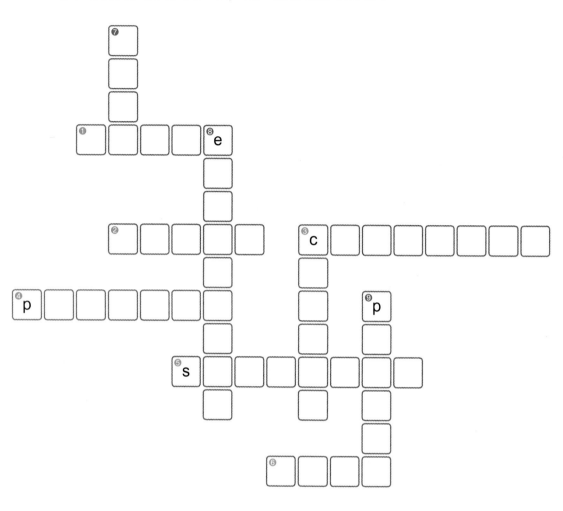

☞ **Across**

❶ A _____ is an activity of buying, selling goods or services.

❷ to make someone do something that he or she does not want to do

❸ the opposite of producer

❹ 농산물: agricultural _____

❺ something that solves a problem

❻ the amount of money that pays for or buy something

Down

❸ a similar word of make or produce

❼ 공정한 경기: _____ game

❽ 대학 교육: university _____

❾ money that is made in a business

B

다음 [보기]에서 알맞은 말을 골라 문장을 완성하시오.

| 보기 | trade | atmosphere | responsibility | profit | consumer |

1 They made a huge _____ from the business.

2 The festival _____ could be felt in the village.

3 American Indians wanted to _____ furs for tools and weapons.

4 Companies should try to respond to _____ demand.

5 You should take _____ for what you have done.

☀ 생각을 키우는 서술형 · 수행평가 대비 훈련

C

다음 [보기]에서 알맞은 말을 골라 글을 완성하시오.

Attention all coffee lovers! Do you like meeting friends and enjoying a cup of coffee? Then I want to share a _____ with you. My vision is a world where coffee _____ and coffee drinkers both enjoy _____ lives. Many small coffee growers today can't _____ the costs. We must take responsibility for this. The answer is the fair trade _____. Next time you buy coffee in a store or stop by Starbucks, make sure you drink fair trade coffee. We should all care about the coffee growers, not just the coffee drinkers!

| 보기 | fair | cover | movement | vision | growers |

UNIT 06 Living in Space

SPACE

#Topic Space, ISS & Astronauts' Life

"지구는 푸른빛이었다."라는 말은 1961년 세계 최초로 spacecraft 를 타고 우주에 간 유리 가가린이라는 astronaut가 남긴 것으로 유명해요. 유리 가가린 이후에 우주 개발이 본격적으로 진행되어 많은 우주 비행사들이 우주에 발을 디딜 수 있었어요. 또한 scientific experiment를 하기 위해 satellite도 우주로 많이 보내져서 현재 4,800여 개가 넘는 satellite가 우주에 float하고 있다고 해요.

우주는 굉장히 위험한 곳이에요. 태양이 비출 때와 비추지 않을 때는 온도가 수백 도의 차이가 나고, 빠른 속도로 날아다니는 우주 먼지도 많아요. 하지만 우주 정거장 안은 공기로 가득 차 있어 특수 equipment가 달린 우주복이 아닌 일상복을 입고 생활을 할 수 있어요. 우주는 무중력 상태이기 때문에 행동이 자유롭지 못해요. 우주에서 오래 생활을 하면 뼈에서 칼슘이, 근육에서는 질소가 빠져나가요. 그래서 우주 비행사들에게 균형 있고 영양가 높은 식단은 필수적이에요.

초기의 음식들은 튜브에 넣어 짜서 먹는 형태로 종류가 다양하지 못했지만 지금은 지상과 비슷한 백여 가지의 음식이 있어요. moisture가 제거된 형태로 돼 있거나, 통조림 형태로 만든 것도 있어요. 우주에서는 먹는 것, 씻는 것, 자는 것 등 모두가 complicated하고 쉽지 않은 일이에요. 그래서 우주에서 지낸다는 것은 단순히 재밌는 일만은 아닌 것 같아요. 국제 우주 정거장에서의 생활은 어떤지 좀 더 구체적으로 알아봐요.

본문 미리보기 QUIZ

1 국제 우주 정거장(ISS)은
☐ 과학 연구를 위해
☐ 관광객 유치 목적으로
개발되었다. 50쪽에서 확인

2 우주에서의 물은 땀에 젖은 옷의 습기조차도
☐ 빨리 버려진다.
☐ 재활용된다. 52쪽에서 확인

☐ 1	**astronaut** [ǽstrənɔ̀ːt]	몡 우주 비행사	여성 우주 비행사	a female _____
☐ 2	**benefit** [bénəfit]	몡 이익	경제적 이익	economic _____
☐ 3	**complicated** [kámpləkèitid]	혱 복잡한	복잡한 일	_____ work
☐ 4	**equipment** [ikwípmənt]	몡 장비	음향 장비	audio _____
☐ 5	**experiment** [ikspérəmənt]	몡 실험	핵 실험	nuclear _____
☐ 6	**float** [flout]	통 떠다니다	물에 뜨다	_____ on water
☐ 7	**headache** [hédèik]	몡 골칫거리, 두통	두통이 있다	have a _____
☐ 8	**maintenance** [méintənəns]	몡 유지	관리비	_____ fee
☐ 9	**moisture** [mɔ́istʃər]	몡 수분	수분을 제거하다	remove _____
☐ 10	**precious** [préʃəs]	혱 소중한	소중한 시간	_____ time
☐ 11	**purpose** [pə́ːrpəs]	몡 목적	고의로	on _____
☐ 12	**satellite** [sǽtəlàit]	몡 위성	기상 위성	a weather _____
☐ 13	**scientific** [sàiəntífik]	혱 과학적인	과학적 방법	a _____ method
☐ 14	**spacecraft** [spéiskræft]	몡 우주선	유인 우주선	a manned _____
☐ 15	**swallow** [swálou]	통 삼키다	쉽게 삼키다	_____ easily

어휘 자신만만 QUIZ

1 우주 비행사들은 우주에서 많은 장비를 착용하고 움직여야 한다.

Astronauts have to move in space with a lot of _____ on.

2 이를 닦고 난 다음에 우주 비행사들은 치약을 삼켜야 한다.

After brushing their teeth, astronauts have to _____ the toothpaste.

Astronauts in the ISS

The International Space Station (ISS) is a large satellite that was developed for the purpose of scientific research. Many astronauts from different countries fly to the ISS and stay from a few days to several months. It is always busy up there. The astronauts work for twelve hours a day.

5 The ISS is like a large, complicated house. Astronauts have to take good care of it. They spend a lot of time doing chores, such as cleaning and maintenance. Getting rid of trash and (A) unloading / to unload fresh supplies are a major part of life in space. Sometimes the astronauts have to work outside the spacecraft to do repairs. Going outside into space can be dangerous. The

10 temperature in space is almost -270℃, and astronauts have to move in space with a lot of equipment on.

Astronauts also spend much of their time preparing and carrying out scientific experiments. They investigate the effects of a weightless environment on materials, plants, and animals. The research findings may improve our

15 knowledge of the natural world and (B) lead / leads to economic and environmental benefits.

Words   satellite 뗑 위성   develop 통 개발하다   purpose 뗑 목적   scientific 뛩 과학적인   research 뗑 조사
astronaut 뗑 우주 비행사 complicated 뛩 복잡한 maintenance 뗑 유지 unload 통 (짐을) 내리다 supply 뗑 공급품
repair 뗑 수리   equipment 뗑 장비   experiment 뗑 실험   investigate 통 조사하다   benefit 뗑 이익

Study Date: _____ / _____

Main Idea

1 글의 요지로 가장 알맞은 것은?

a. Living in space is very dangerous.

b. Astronauts have a busy life on the ISS.

c. Scientific experiments in the ISS are very important.

d. Astronauts have discovered a lot of things about the universe.

Grammar

2 (A)와 (B)에 들어갈 말로 바르게 짝지어진 것은?

	(A)	(B)		(A)	(B)
a.	unloading	…… lead	b.	to unload	…… lead
c.	unloading	…… leads	d.	to unload	…… leads

Details

3 문장을 읽고 본문의 내용과 일치하면 T, 일치하지 않으면 F를 쓰시오.

(1) _____ Astronauts cannot stay more than one month on the ISS.

(2) _____ Astronauts spend a lot of time taking care of the ISS.

(3) _____ Astronauts investigate how a weightless environment affects animals.

Graphic Organizer

4 본문의 단어를 이용하여 표를 완성하시오.

Astronauts' Work in the ISS

Taking care of the ISS	Carrying out scientific _____

• Cleaning and maintenance
  – getting rid of _____
  – unloading fresh _____
• Doing repairs outside the spacecraft
	• Investigating the effects of a _____ situation

지식백과

최초로 우주로 나간 개, 라이카

최초로 우주로 나간 생명체는 무엇일까? 당연히 인간일 것이라고 생각하겠지만, 사실 최초의 우주 여행을 한 생명체는 라이카라는 이름의 개다. 인류 최초의 인공위성은 1957년 발사된 소련의 스푸트니크 1호이며, 한 달 뒤 발사된 스푸트니크 2호 안에는 살아있는 개가 실려 있었다. 동물 단체를 비롯한 여러 사람들의 비판에도 불구하고, 이와 같은 경험을 통해 인류는 실제로 인간을 우주로 내보내기 전 몸에서 어떤 변화가 일어나는지에 대한 귀중한 정보를 얻을 수 있었다.

🕐 My Reading Time | Words 170 / 1분 55초

1회 _____ 분 _____ 초   2회 _____ 분 _____ 초

Staying clean in space is not easy. There is very little water and every drop is precious. _____, water does not "flow" there, but "floats." So, what do people do up there when they have to stay in the ISS for six months at a time?

5 　　To wash themselves, astronauts use special soaps and shampoos which do not need water to rinse. They must use the soaps carefully. If they don't, the soap bubbles will go all over the place. After washing, they use a towel to dry off. Brushing their teeth in space is also a headache. Astronauts use toothpaste and toothbrushes just like the ones on Earth, but there is no sink in the spacecraft. After brushing their teeth, astronauts have to swallow the toothpaste.

10 　　Every bit of water is recycled. Even the moisture in sweaty clothes is taken out and recycled for drinking and other purposes. Astronauts may drink each other's sweat! Does living in space still sound great? Don't forget that it comes at a price.

Words

drop 몡 방울　　precious 혱 소중한　　flow 통 흐르다　　float 통 떠다니다　　at a time 한 번에　　rinse 통 헹구다
headache 몡 골칫거리　　spacecraft 몡 우주선　　sink 몡 싱크대　　swallow 통 삼키다　　bit 몡 조금, 약간
recycle 통 재활용하다　　moisture 몡 수분　　purpose 몡 목적　　sweat 몡 땀　　come at a price 대가가 따르다

1 Topic

This passage is mainly about _____ .

a. how we can keep space clean

b. how water is recycled in space

c. how astronauts drink water in space

d. how astronauts clean themselves in space

2 Linking

Which one best fits in the blank?

a. However

b. Therefore

c. Moreover

d. For example

3 Details

Four astronauts are talking about their lives on the ISS. Which one is NOT true?

a. Nicole: I don't take a shower with running water.

b. John: I don't need water to rinse the shampoo.

c. Yuna: I use a special toothbrush and toothpaste.

d. Naoto: My sweat may be a source of drinking water.

4 Summary

Complete the summary with the words from the passage.

Because there is very little _____ , astronauts have difficulty staying clean in space. They use special soaps and shampoos which do not need water to _____ and use a towel to dry off. They swallow the _____ after brushing their teeth. Moreover, every bit of water is _____ , so astronauts may drink other's _____ .

지식 백과

우주 비행사들의 식사

무중력 상태에서의 식사는 여러 가지 어려움이 있다. 우주 식품은 오래 둬도 부패하지 않도록 철저히 살균해서 미생물을 최소화해야 한다. 우주식의 재료는 되도록 잘게 썰어서 요리하며 급속히 냉동시킨 다음 그대로 특수 건조기에 넣는다. 이와 같이 만든 건조식품은 물에 젖으면 건조 전과 똑같은 맛을 지닌다. 과일이나 생선 등은 캔에 담아 열처리를 한다.

▶ 우주인의 식탁에 관한 동영상을 확인해 보세요. ⏱ Time 6' 40"

A Unit 06에서 학습한 단어를 생각해 보고, 다음 퍼즐을 완성해 보시오.

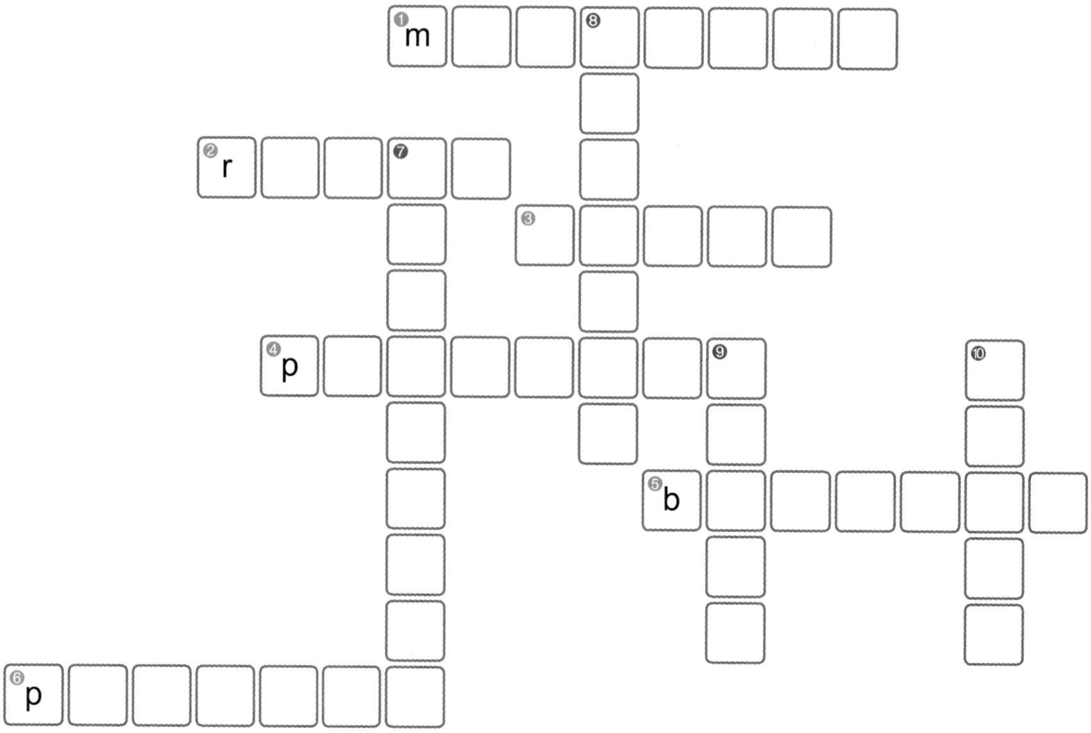

①m □ □ □ ⑧ □ □ □ □ □
②r □ □ ⑦ □ □
③ □ □ □ □ □
④p □ □ □ □ □ □ ⑨ □ ⑩ □
⑤b □ □ □ □ □ □
⑥p □ □ □ □ □ □

☞ Across

❶ 수분을 제거하다: remove _____

❷ to wash something with clean water and without soap

❸ to be carried along by moving water or air

❹ a similar word of valuable or important

❺ A _____ is a good or helpful result or effect.

❻ 고의로: on _____

👇 Down

❼ a machine that is sent into space and that moves around a planet

❽ to take something into your stomach through your mouth and throat

❾ 식은땀: cold _____

❿ 대가가 따르다: come at a _____

B   다음 [보기]에서 알맞은 말을 골라 문장을 완성하시오.

> 보기   float   investigate   maintenance   rinse   supplies

1   The detective will _____ the case closely.

2   The ship is carrying medical _____ for patients.

3   It is hard to understand how boats made of steel _____ on water.

4   When you wash your face, _____ the soap carefully with warm water.

5   The building is closed at present due to _____ work.

☀ 생각을 키우는 서술형 · 수행평가 대비 훈련

C   다음 글을 읽고, 밑줄 친 부분 중 <u>틀린</u> 부분을 찾아 바르게 고치시오.

The new astronaut is ⓐgetting used to daily life in the ISS. In the morning, he washes ⓑhimself, but he must be careful. The soap bubbles from the special soap can go all over the place. He is also careful with water because it is so precious. He learns ⓒto recycle the moisture in sweaty clothes. "Do we drink each other's sweat?" he asks. Later, he spends several hours ⓓcarry out scientific experiments. After that, he is tired, but his day is not finished yet. He must unload fresh supplies and help with many chores. ⓔLiving in space is hard work!

_____ → _____

생각의 폭을 넓히는 배경지식 Story

#*Topic* Disease, Vaccinations & Louis Pasteur

어린 시절 예방 접종을 하기 위해 팔을 걷고 무섭게 생긴 주사 바늘을 기다리며 공포에 떨던 moment가 있죠? 어른이나 아이나 할 것 없이 팔에 주사기를 inject하는 것은 제일 하기 싫은 일 중에 하나인데요. 이제 주사기를 피할 수 있는 solution이 생겼어요. 과학 기술의 발달 덕분에 피부에 붙이는 주사가 곧 나올 거라는 소식이에요. 이제 terrible하게 생긴 주사 바늘과 헤어질 날이 곧 올 것 같아요.

그런데 왜 우리는 예방 접종을 해야 하는 걸까요? 우리 몸에 바이러스가 침투하면 우리 몸은 protect할 준비를 해요. 우리 몸은 한 번 싸워 이긴 바이러스를 아주 잘 기억해서 다시 침입했을 때 항체를 만들어 물리쳐요. 이러한 사실을 이용하여 disease를 prevent할 수 있게 하는 것이 바로 백신이에요. 그래서 백신은 죽거나 약한 바이러스로 만들어요.

백신이 없었던 옛날에는 deadly한 전염병으로 수많은 사람들이 죽었어요. 대표적인 병이 천연두였는데 18세기 영국의 제너 박사가 소의 약한 천연두 균을 천연두 백신으로 사용하기 시작했어요. 이후 이 연구는 파스퇴르에게 큰 영향을 주어 면역학과 백신이 학문으로 정립되는 데 큰 공헌을 했어요. 이어지는 이야기를 통해 파스퇴르가 한 일에 관해 자세히 알아보도록 해요.

본문 미리보기 QUIZ

1 루이 파스퇴르는 [☐ 광견병 / ☐ 소아마비] 백신을 발견했다. 58쪽에서 확인

2 [☐ 백신은 / ☐ 항체는] 약한 병원균을 몸 속에 주사하여 인체의 면역 체계를 활성화 시키는 데 사용한다. 60쪽에서 확인

□ 1	**bite** [bait]	통 물다	손톱을 물어뜯다	_____ one's nails
□ 2	**career** [kəríər]	명 직업, 경력	경력을 쌓다	build one's _____
□ 3	**deadly** [dédli]	형 치명적인	치명적인 병	_____ disease
□ 4	**disease** [dizíːz]	명 질병	피부병	a skin _____
□ 5	**fight off**	…와 싸워 물리치다	죽음과 싸우다	_____ death
□ 6	**heat** [hiːt]	통 뜨겁게 만들다	물을 데우다	_____ water
□ 7	**inject** [indʒékt]	통 주사하다	약물을 주사하다	_____ a drug
□ 8	**mad** [mæd]	형 미친	미치다	go _____
□ 9	**matter** [mǽtər]	명 문제	사적인 문제	private _____
□ 10	**moment** [móumənt]	명 순간	역사적인 순간	a historic _____
□ 11	**prevent** [privént]	통 예방하다	화재를 예방하다	_____ fire
□ 12	**protect** [prətékt]	통 보호하다	자연을 보호하다	_____ nature
□ 13	**solution** [səlùːʃən]	명 해결책	해결책을 찾다	find a _____
□ 14	**stimulate** [stímjulèit]	통 자극하다	호기심을 자극하다	_____ curiosity
□ 15	**terrible** [térəbl]	형 끔찍한	끔찍한 경험	a _____ experience

어휘 자신만만 QUIZ

1 Pasteur 는 질병에 맞서는 백신을 발견했다.

Pasteur had found a vaccine against the _____.

2 그것들은 면역 체계를 자극하게 되고, 면역 체계는 항체를 형성한다.

They _____ the immune system, which makes antibodies.

Louis Pasteur's Great Work

In 1857, a terrible disease killed many sheep and cows in Paris. Louis Pasteur looked into the matter and found something interesting. If an animal survived the disease, it never caught that disease again. Pasteur thought: If I inject a weak form of the disease into healthy animals, they will be _____.

5   His idea worked. The animals never caught the terrible disease. Pasteur had found a vaccine against the disease.

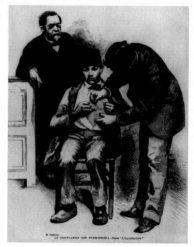

One day in 1885, a doctor brought a boy to Pasteur. The boy's name was Joseph Meister. A mad dog had bitten him, so the doctor thought

10   he would get a deadly disease called *rabies. The doctor took the boy to Pasteur because he was experimenting with a rabies vaccine. Though Pasteur had never tried it on people, he decided to try his vaccine on the boy anyway. The vaccine

15   worked, and the boy lived.

During Pasteur's career, he found many scientific solutions to everyday problems. One of the other problems was milk. People could catch diseases from it. Pasteur found that if he heated the milk, it became safe and could keep it longer than before. Today, thanks to him, many people can enjoy safe

20   milk every day. Remember how we call this safe milk. It's "*pasteurized milk."

* **rabies** 광견병
* **pasteurized** 살균된

Words

terrible 혱 끔찍한 disease 몡 질병 matter 몡 문제 inject 통 주사하다 protect 통 보호하다 vaccine 몡 백신
bite 통 물다 deadly 혱 치명적인 experiment 통 실험을 하다 career 몡 직업, 경력 scientific 혱 과학적인
solution 몡 해결책 heat 통 뜨겁게 만들다 safe 혱 안전한 call 통 …라고 부르다

1 ● Title

본문의 다른 제목으로 가장 알맞은 것은?

a. How to Use Vaccines Effectively

b. Pasteur's Contributions to Medicine and Science

c. Sheep and Cows Are in Need of Vaccines

d. Different Uses of Vaccines and Pasteurized Milk

2 ● Inference

본문의 빈칸에 들어갈 말로 가장 알맞은 것은?

a. killed   b. caught   c. protected   d. left

3 ● Detail

문장을 읽고 본문의 내용과 일치하면 T, 일치하지 않으면 F를 쓰시오.

(1) _____ Louis Pasteur tried his vaccine on animals.

(2) _____ Joseph Meister's doctor was bitten by a mad dog.

(3) _____ Pasteurized milk is safe for people to drink.

4 ● Summery

본문의 단어를 이용하여 요약을 완성하시오.

> Louis Pasteur found a _____ for a disease that killed many animals. By injecting a _____ form of the disease into a healthy animal, he could protect it against the disease. Years later, Pasteur tried his _____ vaccine on a boy who had been bitten by a _____ dog. The boy _____ thanks to Pasteur's vaccine. Pasteur also found that milk became safe when it was _____.

바이러스가 일으키는 병, 감기

지식 백과

감기는 바이러스가 일으키는 대표적인 병이다. 그런데 우리 몸의 면역 체계는 한 번 들어온 항원을 기억하여 항체를 만들어 낼 수 있는데, 감기는 왜 또다시 걸리는 것일까? 사실 감기를 일으키는 바이러스는 200여 종이 넘으며, 이들이 계속 변이를 일으켜 완벽하게 면역이 되는 것은 불가능하다. 외부 바이러스의 침투로 인한 감기의 효과적인 예방법은 외출 후 손을 깨끗하게 씻어 바이러스를 제거하는 것이다.

Reading 02

How Vaccinations Work

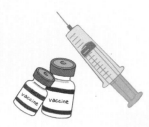

We get injections when we are sick. Sometimes, however, we get injections not to be sick. These injections are called vaccinations. Why do we need them? One painful moment keeps us from getting many diseases. It can save our lives. In fact, vaccinations are the main reasons why people live longer these days.

Vaccines contain forms of bacteria and viruses which cause diseases. These bacteria and viruses are called *pathogens. Pathogens in vaccines are not strong enough to cause diseases. When we get a vaccination, weak pathogens are injected into the body. They stimulate the immune system, which makes antibodies. The formation of these antibodies is the key to preventing diseases in the future. These antibodies will remember how to kill the pathogens. When strong pathogens enter the body, the antibodies will help our body quickly fight them off.

Scientists have developed vaccines for diseases such as *small pox, *chicken pox, *measles, and malaria. In the future, they may be able to develop vaccines for many other diseases. Thanks to vaccines, people live longer, healthier lives.

* **pathogen** 병원균
* **small pox** 천연두
* **chicken pox** 수두
* **measles** 홍역

Words injection 명 주사   vaccination 명 백신 접종   moment 명 순간   contain 동 포함하다   bacteria 명 박테리아, 세균   virus 명 바이러스   stimulate 동 자극하다   immune system 면역 체계   antibody 명 항체   formation 명 형성   prevent 동 예방하다   fight off …와 싸워 물리치다

Topic

1 This passage is mainly about _____.

a. the pain of injections

b. how to live long and healthily

c. principles behind vaccinations

d. the cost of vaccine development

Details

2 Which is NOT true about vaccines?

a. People need vaccines when they are sick.

b. Vaccines help people live longer.

c. Vaccines contain weak forms of pathogens.

d. A vaccine for chicken pox has already been developed.

Process

3 Number the events in order.

☐ You get an injection.

☐ Antibodies are produced.

☐ Weak pathogens stimulate the immune system.

☐ Weak pathogens in a vaccine come into your body.

Graphic Organizer

4 Complete the chart with the words in the passage.

Vaccinations

What is a vaccination?	An _____ that keeps people from getting sick
How do vaccinations work?	1. Weak pathogens are injected into the body. 2. The pathogens stimulate the _____ system. 3. _____ are formed. 4. Antibodies help the body fight _____ pathogens.
What does the future hold?	More _____ will be developed.

지식백과 **천연두의 종말, 우두법 vs. 인두법**

천연두는 300년 전만 해도 가장 무서운 질병 중에 하나였다. 전염성이 강해 한번 유행하면 수천 혹은 수만 명이 목숨을 잃었다. 천연두의 예방법에는 동양에서 처음 시작되어 서양으로 건너간 것으로 알려진 인두법이 있다. 사람의 천연두 바이러스를 접종하는 인두법은 바이러스가 너무 강해서 접종자가 사망할 확률이 높았기 때문에 소의 천연두 바이러스를 이용하여 접종하는 우두법으로 대체되었다. 이 예방법의 발견으로 1979년 세계 보건 기구는 공식적으로 천연두가 지구상에서 사라졌다고 발표하였다.

ⓞ 천연두가 어떻게 정복됐는지 동영상으로 만나 보세요. ⏺ Time 4' 33"

A Unit 07에서 학습한 단어를 생각해 보고, 다음 퍼즐을 완성해 보시오.

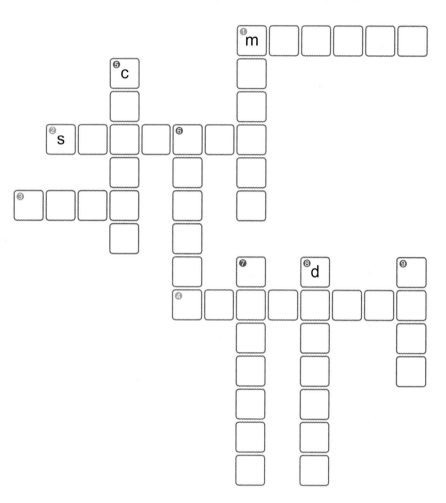

Across

① 사적인 문제: private _____

② the opposite of die

③ 손톱을 물어뜯다: _____ one's nails

④ very bad or unpleasant

Down

① 역사적인 순간: a historic _____

⑤ A _____ is a period of time spent in a job.

⑥ 약물을 주사하다: _____ a drug

⑦ to stop something from happening or existing

⑧ 피부병: a skin _____

⑨ _____ means cause something to become warm or hot.

B 다음 [보기]에서 알맞은 말을 골라 문장을 완성하시오.

> 보기   bite   deadly   experiment   inject   stimulate

1 This camp will _____ public interest in science.

2 Our dog does not _____, so please come in.

3 I _____ed with magnets in science class today.

4 My mom needs to _____ herself every day to cure the disease.

5 Thomas has been fighting a _____ disease for 3 years.

🔆 생각을 키우는 서술형 · 수행평가 대비 훈련

C 다음 [보기]에서 알맞은 말을 골라 글을 완성하시오.

The story of Jospeh Meister is an interesting one. Thanks to his meeting with a mad dog as a child, many lives were saved. After the dog bit him, a doctor took him to Louis Pasteur. Pasteur had not tested his rabies _____ on people, but he did not want to let Joseph die. Pasteur took a _____ pathogen and gave Joseph an injection. The pathogen stimulated his _____ system. It made antibodies to _____ the disease, and Jospeh _____ed. Later, Pasteur helped other people with the vaccine, too.

> 보기   recover   weak   immune   vaccine   fight

#*Topic* Spring, Celebrations & Groundhog Day

길고 severe한 겨울에 지쳐 갈 때쯤이면 사람들은 너 나 할 것 없이 어서 봄이 오기를 고대하게 되죠. 예로부터 우리나라에는 spring이 오는 것을 기념하기 위한 다양한 tradition이 있어요.

우리나라 절기에서 봄의 시작을 indicate하는 날을 '입춘'이라고 해요. 이날이 되면 우리 조상들은 한 해 동안 무탈하고 풍요롭기를 기원하며 대문에 '입춘대길(立春大吉)'의 글귀를 적은 종이를 붙였어요. 이뿐 아니라 다양한 method로 한 해의 길흉을 predict했어요. 입춘날 보리의 뿌리를 캐서 보리 뿌리가 셋이면 풍년이고, 뿌리가 하나이면 흉년이 들 거라고 생각했어요. 또한 입춘날 날씨가 맑고 바람이 없으면 풍년이 들고 생활이 평탄하지만, 이 날 바람이 세고 날씨가 좋지 않으면 흉년이 오고 hardship이 생긴다는 belief도 있었어요.

지금과는 많이 differ한 풍습이지만, 예나 지금이나 봄을 맞이하는 반가운 마음만은 같은 것 같아요. 이어지는 글에서는 봄을 맞이하는 다른 나라의 풍습을 소개하고 있어요. 어떤 재미있는 풍습이 있는지 함께 알아봐요.

본문 미리보기 QUIZ

1 Groundhog Day는 [☐ 북아메리카 / ☐ 남아메리카] 에서 잘 알려진 기념일이다. 74쪽에서 확인

2 옛날 많은 사람들이 [☐ 새싹 / ☐ 달걀] 을 새 생명이나 재생의 상징으로 생각했다. 76쪽에서 확인

□ 1	**assimilate** [əsíməlèit]	통 흡수하다, 동화되다	자연에 동화되다	_____ with nature
□ 2	**belief** [bilí:f]	명 믿음, 신념	강한 신념	a strong _____
□ 3	**contain** [kəntéin]	통 포함하다	카페인을 함유하다	_____ caffeine
□ 4	**destroy** [distrɔ́i]	통 파괴하다	증거를 없애다	_____ evidence
□ 5	**differ** [dífər]	통 다르다	의견을 달리하다	_____ in opinion
□ 6	**frighten** [fráitn]	통 놀라게 하다	쉽게 놀라다	be easily _____ed
□ 7	**hardship** [háːrdʃip]	명 고난, 역경	고난을 겪다	go through _____
□ 8	**hibernate** [háibərnèit]	통 동면하다	겨울에 동면하다	_____ in winter
□ 9	**indicate** [índəkèit]	통 나타내다	출처를 나타내다	_____ the source
□ 10	**method** [méθəd]	명 방법	효과적인 방법	an effective _____
□ 11	**predict** [pridíkt]	통 예측하다	미래를 예측하다	_____ the future
□ 12	**retreat** [ritríːt]	통 뒤로 물러가다	~로부터 물러서다	_____ from
□ 13	**severe** [sivíər]	형 혹독한	혹독한 겨울	a _____ winter
□ 14	**shadow** [ʃǽdəu]	명 그림자	나무의 그림자	the _____ of a tree
□ 15	**tradition** [trədíʃən]	명 전통	전통을 지키다	keep _____

어휘 자신만만 QUIZ

1 겨울에 그라운드호그는 곰처럼 겨울잠을 잔다.

In the winter, a groundhog _____ like a bear.

2 이 관습 중의 많은 것들이 기독교의 부활절 의식에 흡수되었다.

Many of these customs were _____ into the Christian Easter celebration.

🕐 My Reading Time | Words 211 / 2분 20초

| 1회 | 분 | 초 | 2회 | 분 | 초 |

Groundhog Day is a well-known holiday in North America. It is celebrated in the United States and Canada on February 2. According to the weather of the day, people predict whether the cold winter will last longer or the warm spring will soon come.

A groundhog, also known as a woodchuck, is a small animal that digs a 5 hole and lives under the ground. ⓐ It is found across North America. In the winter, ⓑ it hibernates like a bear. ⓒ It is said that the groundhog wakes up from its hibernation and comes up from its hole on February 2. If it is sunny, the groundhog will see its shadow and be frightened. ⓓ It will retreat into its 10 hole and wait for spring. If it is cloudy, it will not see its shadow. Then, it will stay above the ground. Many Americans watch the sky on February 2 and they are happy if it is cloudy. Spring is near!

This method of weather prediction came from the European tradition of 15 Candlemas, which falls on February 2 as well. Good weather at Candlemas is believed to indicate severe winter weather later. This belief was brought to America during the 18th century by German settlers. The settlers later adopted the groundhog as their weather predictor.

Words celebrate 통 축하하다   predict 통 예측하다   last 통 지속하다   dig 통 (땅을) 파다   hibernate 통 동면하다
shadow 명 그림자   frighten 통 놀라게 하다   retreat 통 뒤로 물러가다   method 명 방법   tradition 명 전통
indicate 통 나타내다   severe 형 혹독한   belief 명 믿음, 신념   settler 명 정착민, 이주민   adopt 통 채택하다

1 • Title

두 번째 단락의 제목으로 가장 알맞은 것은?

a. Groundhog Day in North America

b. Why Groundhogs Hibernate in Winter

c. How People Predict Weather on Groundhog Day

d. How German Settlers Brought Their Tradition to America

2 • Details

Groundhogs에 관한 설명 중 본문의 내용과 일치하지 <u>않는</u> 것은?

a. They are also called woodchucks.

b. They live in an underground hole.

c. They are awake only in the spring months.

d. They are believed to wake up on February 2.

3 • Reference

밑줄 친 ⓐ~ⓓ 중 가리키는 대상이 나머지와 <u>다른</u> 것은?

a. ⓐ   b. ⓑ   c. ⓒ   d. ⓓ

4 • Summary

본문의 단어를 이용하여 요약을 완성하시오.

Groundhog Day is _____ in North America on _____ 2 as a day to predict the _____. On this day, it is said that a groundhog wakes up from its _____ and comes out of its underground hole. The groundhog responds to its _____, which helps people predict the weather. The custom came from the European tradition of _____, which was brought to America by _____ settlers.

지식 백과

Groundhog (그라운드호그)

우드척이라고도 불리우며 다람쥐과에 속하는 대형 땅다람쥐의 일종이다. 다른 그라운드호그는 산악 지대에 살지만 우드척은 저지대에 서식한다. 북아메리카에 널리 분포하며 미국 북동부와 중부 지역 및 캐나다에서 흔하게 발견된다. 다 자란 우드척은 꼬리를 합한 길이가 42~51cm 정도 되며, 무게는 2~6kg 정도 된다.

Spring Celebrations

People around the world have always celebrated the coming of spring. For ancient peoples, spring was a time of new hope and new life. When the hardship of winter finally retreated and spring came, they celebrated.

While customs differed in different places, many people thought the egg a
5 symbol of new life or rebirth. The ancient Egyptians and Persians celebrated spring festivals by painting and eating eggs. In ancient Russia, eggs were given as gifts in springtime. According to a Russian myth, the egg contained a source of fire that (A) created / destroyed everything. Many of these customs were assimilated into the Christian Easter celebration. The early Christians
10 adopted the egg as a symbol of the resurrection of Jesus Christ. People decorate eggs and eat them on Easter Day.

Many cultures hold spring celebrations on the spring equinox, which usually (B) falls / reaches around March 20. After that day, the days become longer than the nights. In Japan, it is a national holiday, when families get
15 together and visit their family graves. In many places in Mexico, there are *festivales de primavera* (spring festivals). Children dress up as flowers and animals in parades. Some people visit the ancient city of Teotihuacan. They dress in white and climb to the top of the Pyramid of
20 the Sun for rituals.

Words   ancient 형 고대의   hardship 명 고난, 역경   differ 동 다르다   gift 명 선물   myth 명 신화
contain 동 포함하다   source 명 원천   destroy 동 파괴하다   custom 명 관습   assimilate 동 흡수하다
resurrection 명 부활   equinox 명 낮과 밤의 길이가 같은 날   reach 동 도달하다   ritual 명 의식

Study Date: /

Main Idea

1

Why do people celebrate the coming of spring?

→ They think that spring is a time of _____.

Words

2

Choose the words that fit in boxes (A) and (B).

	(A)		(B)		(A)		(B)
a.	created	·····	falls	b.	created	·····	reaches
c.	destroyed	·····	falls	d.	destroyed	·····	reaches

Details

3

Which is NOT true about the spring equinox?

a. Before that day, the nights are longer than the days.

b. It is a national holiday in Mexico.

c. Japanese usually visit their family graves on that day.

d. On that day, Mexican children dress up and parade around.

Graphic Organizer

4

Complete the map using the information in the passage.

Spring Celebrations

Egg - Symbol of new _____	• Ancient Egyptians and Persians painted and _____ eggs. • Ancient Russians gave eggs as _____. • People decorate and eat eggs on _____ Day.
Spring Equinox - _____ 20	• Japanese families get together and visit their family _____. • Mexicans enjoy spring _____.

봄의 시작, 입춘

지식백과

입춘은 24절기 중 첫 절기로 보통 양력 2월 4일경에 해당한다. 이날부터 새해의 봄이 시작된다. 우리 조상들은 이날을 기리고 일 년 동안 복이 가득하기를 기원하는 갖가지 의례들을 행했다. 흙으로 소 모양을 만들어 문밖에 내어 놓으면 겨울의 추운 기운을 내보낸다고 믿었다. 또한 추위를 견뎌내며 돋아난 햇나물을 이용한 전통 음식을 입춘의 뜻을 기리며 먹는 풍속이 있었다.

▶ 우리 조상들의 입춘 풍속을 동영상으로 알아 보세요. ● Time 3' 43''

A Unit 08에서 학습한 단어를 생각해 보고, 다음 퍼즐을 완성해 보시오.

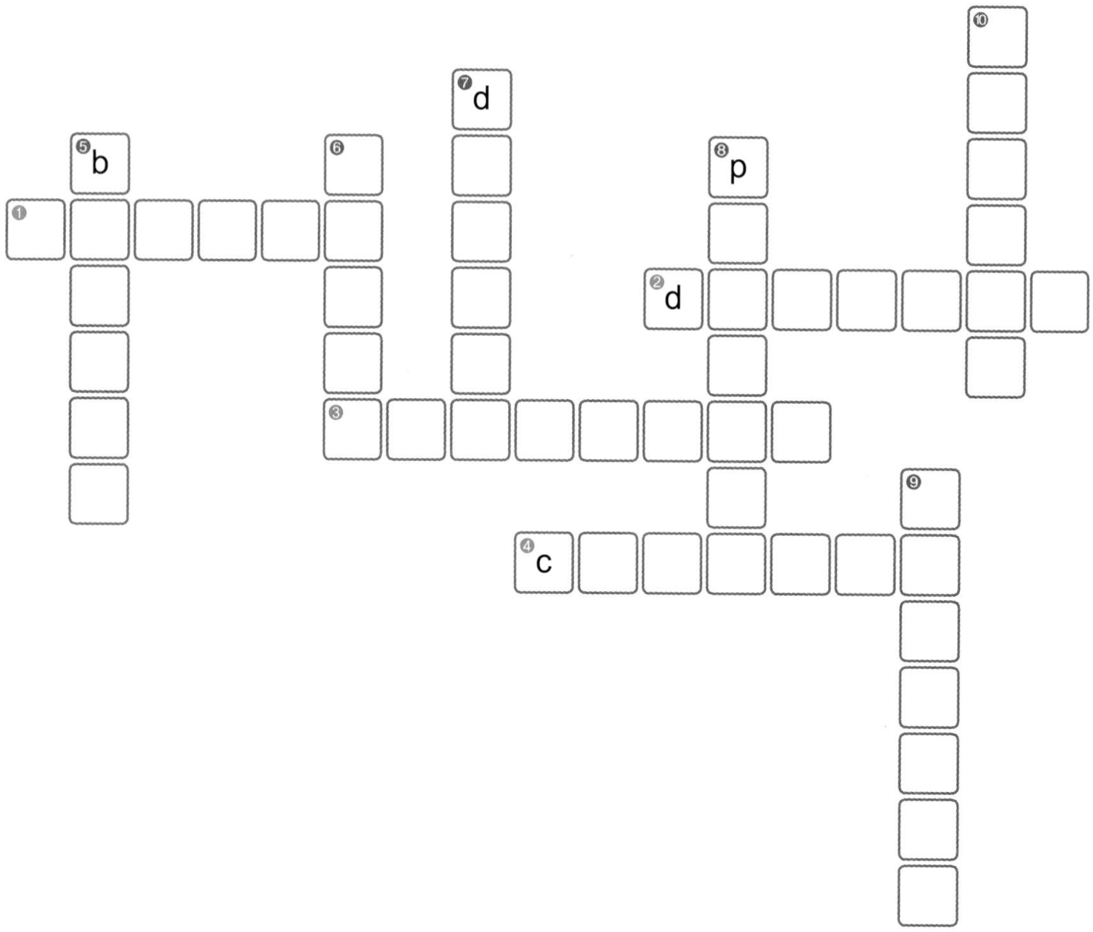

☞ **Across**

❶ very bad, serious, or unpleasant

❷ the opposite of build

❸ pain and suffering

❹ to have something inside

Down

❺ 강한 신념: a strong _____

❻ 육지에 도달하다: _____ land

❼ 의견을 달리하다: _____ in opinion

❽ to say that something will or might happen in the future

❾ 고대인들: _____ peoples

❿ A _____ is a way of doing something.

B 다음 [보기]에서 알맞은 말을 골라 문장을 완성하시오.

보기   hardship   celebrate   retreat   indicate   assimilated

1 These changes were gradually _____ into everyday life.

2 Many people are suffering economic _____.

3 The festival is to _____ Thailand's New Year.

4 The general ordered his troops to _____.

5 The figures _____ that the birth rate has decreased rapidly.

🔆 생각을 키우는 서술형 · 수행평가 대비 훈련

C 다음 글을 읽고, 밑줄 친 부분 중 어색한 부분을 찾아 바르게 고치시오.

Kate is a teacher. The children in her class come from many different countries, including Mexico, Russia, and the United States. Spring is coming, and she decides how her class will ⓐcelebrate. In February, they will celebrate Groundhog Day. They will watch the sky and try to ⓑprevent if winter will last longer or not. ⓒLater, in March, they will learn about the spring equinox. She will let the children dress up as flowers and animals. Finally, the class will bring eggs to class. They will ⓓdecorate the eggs and eat them. Kate hopes the children will ⓔenjoy celebrating spring.

_____ → _____

#Topic Elevator & Space Elevator

승강기가 발명되기 이전에 지을 수 있는 건물의 높이는 최고 5~6층이었다고 해요. 더 높은 건물을 지을 수 있었지만 건물 내의 이동 시간이나 체력 소모를 생각해 보면 inefficient한 일이였어요. 승객용 승강기가 건물에 equip되면서 초고층 건물이 increase하게 되었어요.

승강기를 operate하는 가장 기본적인 device는 도르래예요. 그리스의 아르키메데스가 처음 만든 도르래는 무거운 물체를 손쉽게 raise할 수 있었어요. 그는 도르래를 이용하여 multiple한 짐을 실은 배를 항구로 끌어 왔다고 해요. 이후 그는 물건뿐만 아니라 사람도 convey하는 것이 가능하지 않을까라는 생각을 했어요. 이것이 사람을 들어 올리는 승강기의 시초가 되었죠.

우리나라에 현대식 승강기가 처음 설치된 곳은 1910년 조선은행이었어요. 이때는 화폐 운반용으로 만들어졌다고 해요. 승객용 승강기로는 1914년 철도 호텔에 처음 설치되었어요. 그 당시 승강기는 놀라운 문명이여서 신발을 벗고 탔다고 describe되어 있어요. 지금은 승강기를 탈 때 신발을 벗고 타는 친구는 없겠죠? 이어지는 글을 통해 현대식 승강기의 개발에 큰 공헌을 한 사람에 대해 알아봐요.

〈아르키메데스의 도르래 실험〉

본문 미리보기 QUIZ

1   Elisha Otis는 1861년 [☐ 수력 승강기 / ☐ 증기 승강기] 의 특허를 받았다. 74쪽에서 확인

2   우주 정거장에서 우주 승강기 실험을 한 나라는 [☐ 미국 / ☐ 일본] 이다. 76쪽에서 확인

☐ 1	**announce** [ənáuns]	통 발표하다	계획을 발표하다	_____ a plan
☐ 2	**contrast** [kántræst]	명 대조	선명한 대조	strong _____
☐ 3	**convey** [kənvéi]	통 운반하다	철도로 운반하다	_____ by rail
☐ 4	**describe** [diskráib]	통 묘사하다	상세하게 묘사하다	_____ in detail
☐ 5	**device** [diváis]	명 장치, 기구	안전 장치	safety _____
☐ 6	**enemy** [énəmi]	명 적	적으로 만들다	make an _____
☐ 7	**equip** [ikwíp]	통 장비를 갖추다	…를 위해 갖추다	_____ for
☐ 8	**increase** [inkríːs]	통 증가하다	가격을 올리다	_____ the price
☐ 9	**inefficient** [ìnifíʃənt]	형 비효율적인	비효율적인 방법	_____ ways
☐ 10	**multiple** [mʌ́ltəpl]	형 많은, 다수의	다문화	_____ culture
☐ 11	**operate** [ápərèit]	통 작동하다	기계를 작동하다	_____ a machine
☐ 12	**patent** [pǽtənt]	통 특허를 받다	발명품 특허를 받다	_____ an invention
☐ 13	**primitive** [prímətiv]	형 원시적인	원시 종족	_____ tribes
☐ 14	**raise** [reiz]	통 들어 올리다	손을 들다	_____ hands
☐ 15	**transparent** [trænspɛ́ərənt]	형 투명한	투명한 유리	_____ glass

어휘 자신만만 QUIZ

1 원시적인 승강기는 기원전 3세기만큼이나 일찍 사용되었다.

_____ elevators were in use as early as the 3rd century BC.

2 이와는 대조적으로, 승강기는 그렇게 많은 연료를 들이지 않고도 반복해서 사용될 수 있다.

In _____, elevators can be used again and again without as much fuel.

Who Invented the Elevator?

Modern elevators are amazing. In one hotel in Germany, for example, you can go up and down in a fish tank. The elevator is in the middle of a tube of water containing many sea animals. If glass walls are not enough, try Sky Tower in New Zealand. It takes you straight to the top in 40 seconds — on a

5 transparent floor! It seems elevators are all around us.

Like many other inventions, however, elevators started out simple. Primitive elevators were in use as early as the 3rd century BC. They were platforms operated by human, animal, or waterwheel power. They were used to lift heavy objects like big blocks of stone. An elevator-like lifting device was described in

10 a book in the year 1,000. It was used to raise a large weapon to attack an enemy. From the mid-19th century, power elevators, often steam-operated, were used for conveying materials in factories, mines, and warehouses.

In 1853, American inventor Elisha Otis demonstrated a freight elevator equipped with a safety brake to prevent falling _____ a supporting cable

15 breaks. This increased public confidence in elevators. Otis established a company for manufacturing elevators and patented a steam elevator in 1861. Electric elevators came into use several decades later.

Words

transparent 휑 투명한 primitive 휑 원시적인 operate 통 작동하다 waterwheel 명 물레바퀴 device 명 장치
describe 통 묘사하다 raise 통 들어 올리다 enemy 명 적 convey 통 운반하다 demonstrate 통 입증하다
freight 명 화물 equip 통 장비를 갖추다 increase 통 증가하다 confidence 명 자신감 patent 통 특허를 받다

1 Title

본문의 다른 제목으로 가장 알맞은 것은?

a. The Science of Elevators

b. A Short History of Elevators

c. Different Types of Elevators

d. How to Invent an Elevator

2 Linking

본문의 빈칸에 들어갈 말로 가장 알맞은 것은?

a. in case　　　　　　　　b. unless

c. despite　　　　　　　　d. so that

3 Details

문장을 읽고 본문의 내용과 일치하면 T, 일치하지 않으면 F를 쓰시오.

(1) _____ In the 3rd century BC, the elevators were shaped like a box.

(2) _____ Some of the earlier elevators were often used to lift heavy things.

(3) _____ Elisha Otis patented an electric elevator in 1861.

4 Summary

본문의 단어를 이용하여 요약을 완성하시오.

> Elevators have made our lives more convenient, and faster and safer ones are being developed. Primitive elevators in the _____ century BC were much simpler than today's elevators. They were just _____ powered in different ways. A safer elevator was demonstrated in the _____ century by _____ _____. He equipped his elevator with a safety brake. Electric elevators appeared at the end of the 19th century.

지식백과

줄이 없는 자기 부상 승강기 (MULTI)

160여년 전 승강기가 처음 등장한 이후 승강기의 이동 속도는 빨라졌지만 수직 이동하는 방식에는 변함이 없었다. 또한 승강기 케이블의 무게 때문에 실제로 승강기는 500m를 초과하여 설치할 수 없었다. 세계에서 제일 높은 건물인 부르즈 칼리파는 828m로, 이 건물을 오르려면 승강기를 43층, 76층, 124층에서 갈아타야 한다. 하지만 새롭게 개발된 자기 부상 승강기는 상하좌우로도 움직임이 가능하고 수송 능력 증가, 전력과 승강기 공간 감소 등 고층 건물에 큰 변화를 가져 올 것이다.

Up, Up and Away

Imagine sitting in an elevator car, riding far up into space on a cable. Does it sound like science fiction? Actually, many scientists predict that space elevators will become a

5   reality within our lifetime. In fact, one company in Japan announced plans to make a space elevator by 2050. In 2018, elevator experiments started at the international space station.

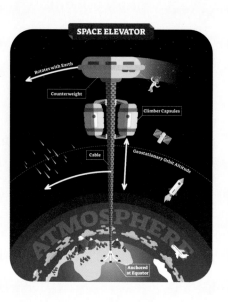

10   Many people don't realize how (A) inefficient / efficient rocket travel is. Rockets may not be the best way to get into space. The reasons are many. First of all, rockets can hold only a few people or objects, and only some of them can be used multiple times. They also require a lot of fuel. This means that getting into space with a rocket costs a great deal. In contrast, elevators can be

15   used again and again without as much fuel. The concept is simple. There is a space station on one end and Earth on the other. People travel up and down between them on a cable.

Do you still think it is unrealistic? Then remember what people used to say about flying in the air. They said, "It's impossible! Only birds fly!" Yet, today,

20   (B) countable / countless people fly in airplanes every day.

Words   science fiction 공상 과학 소설   predict ⑧ 예상하다   reality ⑲ 현실   announce ⑧ 발표하다   realize ⑧ 깨닫다   inefficient ⑱ 비효율적인   multiple ⑱ 많은, 다수의   require ⑧ 필요로 하다   fuel ⑲ 연료   contrast ⑲ 대조   unrealistic ⑱ 비현실적인   impossible ⑱ 불가능한   countless ⑱ 셀 수 없는

Study Date: _____ / _____

• Main Idea

1 What is the main idea of the passage?

a. Experiments on space elevators are increasing.

b. Space elevators will be a reality in the future.

c. Elevators are used to lift heavy objects.

d. Rockets are the best way to travel space.

• Details

2 Which is NOT true according to the passage?

a. Experiments for space elevators started in 2018.

b. Getting into space with a rocket costs a lot.

c. Elevators require more fuel than rockets.

d. Elevators can be used multiple times.

• Words

3 Choose the words that fit in boxes (A) and (B).

(A)	(B)		(A)	(B)
a. inefficient	⋯⋯ countable		b. inefficient	⋯⋯ countless
c. efficient	⋯⋯ countable		d. efficient	⋯⋯ countless

• Graphic Organizer

4 Complete the map with the words from the passage.

Ways to get into space

Space _____	Rockets
• can be used many times	• can _____ a few people or objects
• do not use as much _____	• _____ a lot of fuel
• connect the _____ _____ and Earth	• _____ a great deal

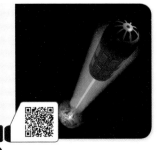

A Unit 09에서 학습한 단어를 생각해 보고, 다음 퍼즐을 완성해 보시오.

☞ Across

❶ 기계를 작동하다: _____ a machine

❷ 발명품 특허를 받다: _____ an invention

❸ too many to be counted

❹ 다문화: _____ cultures

❺ goods that are carried by ships, trains, trucks, or airplanes

👇 Down

❸ 철도로 운반하다: _____ by rail

❻ to provide someone with necessary materials or supplies

❼ the opposite of fantasy

❽ someone who attacks or tries to harm another

❾ a similar word of lift

B 다음 [보기]에서 알맞은 말을 골라 문장을 완성하시오.

보기   primitive   confidence   countless   transparent   inefficient

1 The man will complete the project with great _____.

2 Some scientists argue that there are _____ forms of life on Mars.

3 The container is _____, so you can see what is inside.

4 The system is so _____ that they want to change it.

5 There are _____ stars shining in each galaxy.

🔆 생각을 키우는 서술형 · 수행평가 대비 훈련

C 다음 [보기]에서 알맞은 말을 골라 글을 완성하시오.

A change in planet-to-space transportation will become a _____ in our lifetime. Many people think rockets are the best way to go to space. However, do you realize how _____ rockets are? They hold only a few people and use a great deal of fuel. Instead, I think the space elevator is the _____. The _____ is simple. The elevator car travels up and down on a cable from one end on the space station to the other end on Earth. It can take you to space again and again without much _____. I don't think it still sounds like science fiction.

보기   concept   future   inefficient   reality   fuel

#*Topic* BookCrossing & Fantasy Novel

영화 「해리포터」, 「반지의 제왕」, 「트와일라잇」의 공통점은 무엇일까요? 모두 fantasy 소설을 원작으로 하는 영화라는 점이죠. 어떤 사람들에게는 영화가 더 친숙할 수도 있겠지만, 사실 소설도 영화 못지않게 큰 인기를 누렸어요. 그 중 J. K. 롤링의 해리포터 시리즈는 어른과 어린이 모두를 fascinate한 대표적인

fantasy 소설이에요. 그 인기는 전 세계적으로 대단해서 약 80개의 언어로 translate되었다고 해요. 뿐만 아니라 소설을 바탕으로 만든 영화가 release되고 흥행에 크게 성공하면서 해리포터 시리즈는 엄청난 신드롬을 만들어 냈죠.

아마 여러분 중에도 「해리포터」 영화와 소설을 모두 본 사람이 있을 거예요. 소설을 읽고 나서 영화를 봤을 때, 혹시 여러분의 imagination과는 달라서 실망하지는 않았나요? 책을 읽는 것과 영화를 보는 것 모두가 흥미로운 일이지만, 책이 우리에게 inspire하는 것과 영화는 분명히 다른 점이 있죠. 상상 속에서 나만의 세계를 만들어 내는 것은 영화의 컴퓨터 그래픽으로 흉내 낼 수 없는 일이니까요.

여러분의 상상력을 일깨워 줄 책이 필요하다면 지금 community의 도서관을 방문해 보세요. 또한 자신이 읽은 책을 stranger와 share하는 방법도 있다고 해요. 어떻게 공유하는지 함께 알아봐요.

본문 미리보기 QUIZ

1 BookCrossing은 ⎡ ☐ 중고 책을 사고파는 ⎤ 운동이다. 82쪽에서 확인
⎣ ☐ 책을 나눠 읽는 ⎦

2 판타지 소설은 ⎡ ☐ 흥미진진한 상상의 세계를 탐험할 수 있다. ⎤ 84쪽에서 확인
⎣ ☐ 작가의 경험을 바탕으로 쓰인 글이다. ⎦

□	1	**appeal** [əpíːl]	통 관심을 끌다	십 대의 관심을 끌다	_____ to teens
□	2	**community** [kəmjúːnəti]	명 공동체, 지역 사회	농업 공동체	a farming _____
□	3	**escape** [iskéip]	명 탈출	탈출 경로	an _____ route
□	4	**explore** [iksplɔ́ːr]	통 탐험하다	우주를 탐험하다	_____ space
□	5	**fantasy** [fǽntəsi]	명 공상	공상 소설	_____ novel
□	6	**fascinate** [fǽsənèit]	통 마음을 사로잡다	관중을 사로잡다	_____ the audience
□	7	**identification** [aidèntifəkéiʃən]	명 식별	식별 번호	_____ number
□	8	**imagination** [imæ̀dʒənéiʃən]	명 상상	상상력이 풍부하다	be full of _____
□	9	**inspire** [inspáiər]	통 영감을 주다	작가들에게 영감을 주다	_____ writers
□	10	**practice** [prǽktis]	명 실행, 연습	소방 훈련	fire _____
□	11	**register** [rédʒistər]	통 등록하다	출생 신고를 하다	_____ a birth
□	12	**release** [rilíːs]	통 방출하다	새를 놓아주다	_____ a bird
□	13	**require** [rikwáiər]	통 필요하다	경험이 필요하다	_____ experience
□	14	**share** [ʃɛər]	통 공유하다	음악을 공유하다	_____ the music
□	15	**translate** [trænsléit]	통 번역하다	책을 번역하다	_____ a book

어휘 자신만만 QUIZ

1 독서가들의 이 공동체의 일원이 되어 보아라.

Become a part of this _____ of readers.

2 그 책들은 수십 가지의 언어로 번역되었다.

The books have been _____ into dozens of languages.

Sharing Books with People

⏱ My Reading Time | Words 201 / 2분 12초

1회 _____ 분 _____ 초   2회 _____ 분 _____ 초

There is an interesting way to take care of the books you don't need anymore. You can leave them somewhere, and they may be picked up and read by others. This practice of "BookCrossing" was started by Ron Hornbaker in the U.S. in 2001. He created the website bookcrossing.com, which helps

5 people share books with friends and even total strangers. It had almost two million members in 2018.

It is simple to join this network. To leave or "release" a book somewhere, log on to the website and register the book. (A) Note where and when it will be released, and then go out to release it. (B) Members can search the website

10 for books released in their area, and then go hunting. (C) He or she must enter the book's identification number and information about where and when it was picked up. (D) After it has been read, the book should be released again for someone else to read.

Become a part of this community of readers. There are several benefits to

15 BookCrossing. First, you can enjoy books for free. Also, you can share your books with others. Finally, you can help save trees.

Words   somewhere 튀 어딘가에 pick up ⋯을 줍다 practice 몡 실행, 연습 share 됭 공유하다 stranger 몡 낯선 사람 release 됭 방출하다 log on 접속하다 register 됭 등록하다 note 됭 적다 go hunting 사냥하러 가다 identification 몡 식별 information 몡 정보 community 몡 공동체, 지역 사회

Study Date: _____ / _____

Title

1 각 단락과 요지를 연결하시오.

(1) Paragraph 1 •　　　　　　　　• a. Good Things About BookCrossing

(2) Paragraph 2 •　　　　　　　　• b. A Definition of BookCrossing

(3) Paragraph 3 •　　　　　　　　• c. The Processes of BookCrossing

Organization

2 주어진 문장이 들어가기에 가장 알맞은 곳은?

> A person who picks up a book must visit the website.

a. (A)　　　　　　b. (B)　　　　　　c. (C)　　　　　　d. (D)

Details

3 문장을 읽고 본문의 내용과 일치하면 T, 일치하지 않으면 F를 쓰시오.

(1) _____ BookCrossing was started by Ron Hornbaker.

(2) _____ BookCrossing started with almost two million members.

(3) _____ BookCrossing helps members release or hunt for books.

Graphic Organizer

4 본문의 단어를 이용하여 BookCrossing의 과정을 완성하시오.

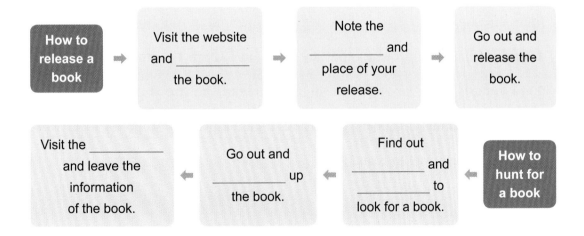

How to release a book ⇒ Visit the website and _____ the book. ⇒ Note the _____ and place of your release. ⇒ Go out and release the book.

Visit the _____ and leave the information of the book. ⇐ Go out and _____ up the book. ⇐ Find out _____ and _____ to look for a book. ⇐ How to hunt for a book

지식백과

세계 책의 날

세계 책의 날은 1995년 유네스코가 세계인의 독서 증진을 위해 정한 날로 매년 4월 23일이다. 이날로 정한 것은 책을 사는 사람들에게 꽃을 선물하는 스페인의 세인트 조지의 날(St. George's Day)에서 유래됐으며 세르반테스와 셰익스피어가 사망한 날이기도 하다. 현재 전 세계적으로 80여 개의 국가에서 세계 책의 날을 기념하고 있다.

▶ 조선 시대에는 책이 어떻게 유통되었는지 동영상으로 알아 보세요. ● Time 5' 07"

Teens and Fantasies

⏱ My Reading Time | Words 197 / 2분 10초

1회 ____분 ____초   2회 ____분 ____초

Some people think ⓐ that teens don't read at all these days. This isn't true, however. A recent survey of U.S. teens shows ⓑ that almost 43% of them read for fun in their free time. This means ⓒ that many teens do reading ⓓ that is not required for schoolwork.

Novels, especially fantasies, are popular among teens around the world. C. S. Lewis's *Chronicles of Narnia* and J. K. Rowling's *Harry Potter* books, for example, top the lists of teens' favorite books. They have been translated into dozens of languages and also made into movies. One student says, "I don't feel like reading newspapers or magazines. But I can't live without fantasies."

Why are teens so fascinated with fantasies? The answer lies in the fact that the genre itself is appealing to teens. In a fantasy, anything can happen, and there are cool characters. Stories are often inspired by mythology; the stories are full of magic and events that are possible only in the imagination. So, a good fantasy allows people to easily forget about the stressful real world and explore an exciting, imaginary one. Fantasies are a perfect escape for teens who are looking for a way to relax.

Words survey 몡 조사   require 통 필요하다   novel 몡 소설   fantasy 몡 공상   translate 통 번역하다
fascinate 통 마음을 사로잡다   appeal 통 관심을 끌다   character 몡 등장인물   inspire 통 영감을 주다
mythology 몡 신화   imagination 몡 상상   allow 통 허락하다   explore 통 탐험하다   escape 몡 탈출

1
・Main Idea

What is the main idea of the passage?

a. Fantasies are popular among readers of all ages.

b. Many teens buy books written by C. S. Lewis and J. K. Rowling.

c. Today's teens read more fantasies than teens in the past.

d. Teens love fantasies because they can experience exciting new worlds.

2
・Details

Which is NOT true according to the passage?

a. The survey results show many teens read for fun.

b. C. S. Lewis and J. K. Rowling are very popular among teens.

c. Teens also like to read magazines and newspapers.

d. Teens' favorite books are often based on mythology.

3
・Grammar

Which underlined that functions differently from the others?

a. ⓐ   b. ⓑ   c. ⓒ   d. ⓓ

4
・Summary

Complete the summary with the words from the passage.

According to a recent survey, many _____ read books for _____. _____ are popular among teens, and books by C. S. Lewis and _____ are many of teens' favorite ones. Teens love to read fantasies because they can meet cool _____ and experience a world that is different from the stressful real world — an exciting, _____ world where anything can happen.

반지의 제왕과 프로도 효과

지식백과

가장 널리 알려진 판타지 소설 중 하나는 「반지의 제왕(The Lord of the Rings)」이다. 본래 J. R. R. 톨킨의 3부작 소설로, 전 세계 38개 이상의 언어로 번역될 만큼 큰 인기를 끌었다. 이후 3부작 영화로 재탄생하면서 또다시 엄청난 관심을 받았는데, 영화의 촬영지였던 뉴질랜드가 관광지로 급부상하는 결과로 이어졌다. 이후 영화 산업에 의해 얻게 되는 부수적인 경제적 이익을 「반지의 제왕」 영화 주인공의 이름을 따서 '프로도 효과'라고 부르게 되었다.

A Unit 10에서 학습한 단어를 생각해 보고, 다음 퍼즐을 완성해 보시오.

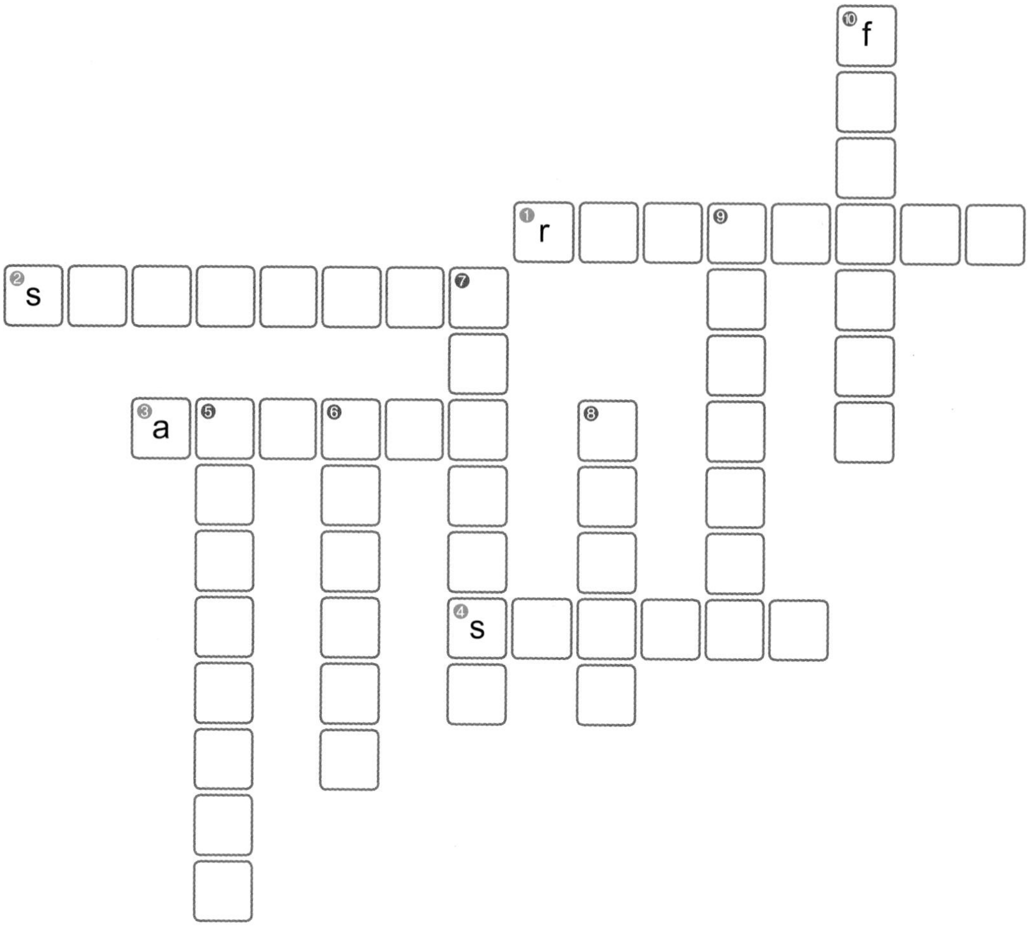

👉 **Across**

❶ 출생 신고를 하다: _____ a birth

❷ A _____ is someone who you have not met before or do not know.

❸ a similar word of fascinate

❹ 시장 조사: market _____

👇 **Down**

❺ the activity of doing something again and again to become better at it

❻ an act getting away from a place where you are being held or kept

❼ 새를 놓아주다: _____ a bird

❽ to have or use something with others

❾ 십 대에 영감을 주다: _____ teens

❿ 공상 소설: _____ novel

B 다음 [보기]에서 알맞은 말을 골라 문장을 완성하시오.

보기	require	register	inspire	practice	escape

1 You need to _____ first in order to use our services fully.

2 These positions _____ fluency in both oral and written English.

3 He had a narrow _____ from the burning building.

4 The idea was so good that the CEO decided to put it into _____.

5 She was glad that she could _____ the graduating students at the ceremony.

💡 생각을 키우는 서술형 · 수행평가 대비 훈련

C 다음 글을 읽고, 밑줄 친 부분 중 틀린 부분을 찾아 바르게 고치시오.

Are you looking for the perfect escape? Then read J. K. Rowling's *Harry Potter* books. They ⓐare popular with teens all over the world. I don't often ⓑfeel like reading magazines, or reading for school, but I love these books. Now I am ⓒfinished to read them, so I will release them. Are you ready to go hunting? You must search behind the community center. The identification number of each book is on the back of the book. Remember to visit the website after you ⓓpick one up. I am waiting to see ⓔwho finds my books!

_____ → _____

생각의 폭을 넓히는 배경지식 Story

#*Topic* Naming, Culture & English Surnames

이름은 단순히 호칭의 의미를 넘어 그 사람만의 고유하고 특별한 존재로서의 의미까지 연결되곤 해요. 그래서 누군가의 characteristic을 나타내는 이름을 짓는다는 것은 참 중요하고 어려운 일인 것 같아요.

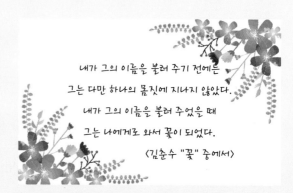

내가 그의 이름을 불러 주기 전에는
그는 다만 하나의 몸짓에 지나지 않았다.
내가 그의 이름을 불러 주었을 때
그는 나에게로 와서 꽃이 되었다.
〈김춘수 "꽃" 중에서〉

모든 부모들은 자녀의 이름을 지을 때, 그들의 소망과 기대를 담아 common한 이름이 아닌 멋진 이름을 지으려고 고민하는데요. 각 culture마다 특별한 custom들이 있어서 보통 그것에 따라 이름을 지어요. 이름은 부모가 자유롭게 짓는 반면 family name은 조상으로부터 물려받기도 하고 어떤 문화에서는 성이 아예 없고 이름만 쓰기도 해요. 우리나라에도 성이 없었던 적이 있었다고 해요. Record에 따르면 삼국시대부터 귀족과 왕족 계층에서만 성을 사용했고, 고려시대가 돼서야 일반인들도 성을 사용했다고 해요.

북아메리카의 인디언들은 자연 현상이나 어떤 circumstance의 특징을 잡아서 이름을 짓는다고 해요. '머리에 부는 바람', '달과 함께 걷다', '발로 차는 새', '주먹 쥐고 일어서' 등이 있어요. 아주 근사하고 unique하지 않나요? 이어지는 글을 통해 나라별로 이름 짓는 풍습에 대해 좀 더 알아봐요.

본문 미리보기 QUIZ

1 말레이시아인들은 대부분 [☐ basket name이 있다. / ☐ 이름에 성이 없다.] 90쪽에서 확인

2 Easter라는 영어 이름의 성은 [☐ 동쪽에서 살고 있다는 / ☐ 직업이 대장장이라는] 것에서 유래했다. 92쪽에서 확인

독해의 장벽을 깨는 만만한 Vocabulary

Date: _____ / _____

☐ 1	**characteristic** [kæ̀riktərístik]	명 특징	가족의 특징	a family _____
☐ 2	**circumstance** [sə́:rkəmstæns]	명 상황	경제적 상황	economical _____
☐ 3	**common** [kámən]	형 흔한	흔한 이름	a _____ name
☐ 4	**compose** [kəmpóuz]	통 구성하다	…로 구성되어 있다	be _____ of
☐ 5	**culture** [kʌ́ltʃər]	명 문화	음식 문화	food _____
☐ 6	**custom** [kʌ́stəm]	명 관습, 풍습	지방의 관습	a local _____
☐ 7	**neighbor** [néibər]	명 이웃	좋은 이웃	a good _____
☐ 8	**occupation** [àkjəpéiʃən]	명 직업	직업을 바꾸다	change one's _____
☐ 9	**official** [əfíʃəl]	형 공식적인	공식 언어	_____ language
☐ 10	**population** [pàpjuléiʃən]	명 인구	인구 증가	_____ growth
☐ 11	**record** [rékərd]	명 기록	기록을 깨다	break the _____
☐ 12	**sibling** [síbliŋ]	명 형제자매	손위 형제자매	older _____
☐ 13	**suppose** [səpóuz]	통 가정하다	…라고 가정하자	Let's _____ that ...
☐ 14	**tricky** [tríki]	형 힘든, 곤란한	곤란한 상황	a _____ situation
☐ 15	**unique** [ju:ní:k]	형 독특한, 특별한	특별한 재능	a _____ talent

어휘 자신만만 QUIZ

1 아기 이름을 짓는 풍습은 문화마다 다르다.

_____ for naming babies vary across cultures.

2 다른 사람들은 직업에 근거하여 성을 지었다.

Others created surnames based on their _____.

Customs for naming babies vary across cultures. In the African-American Gullah community, for example, babies are given both an official name and a basket name. A basket is a cradle for holding a baby. The basket name is usually chosen based on the circumstances of the baby's birth. If a child was born on a Friday, its basket name could be Friday. Within the community, people refer to each other by their basket names, and often don't know each other's official names.

Another unique naming custom is found in Malaysia. Many Malays don't have family names. Instead, men add their father's name to their own name with the term "bin," which means "son of." So, Rosli bin Suleiman would be Rosli the son of Suleiman. _____, women use the term "bint," which means "daughter of." So, Aysha bint Suleiman is Aysha the daughter of Suleiman.

In Korea, most people have a given name composed of two syllables. Siblings often share a syllable. For example, brothers Kim Jeong-min and Kim Jeong-su share the syllable "jeong" in their given names. (Kim is their family name.) However, this practice is becoming less common.

Words   custom 뗑 관습   across 뛰 건너서, 가로질러   culture 뗑 문화   official 뗺 공식적인   cradle 뗑 아기 침대   circumstance 뗑 상황   refer to …로 부르다   unique 뗺 독특한, 특별한   term 뗑 용어   compose 뙇 구성하다   syllable 뗑 음절   sibling 뗑 형제자매   share 뙇 공유하다   common 뗺 흔한

Topic

1 본문의 주제로 가장 알맞은 것은?

a. unique baby names

b. different naming customs

c. the circumstances of babies' births

d. the meanings of family names

Inference

2 다음을 읽고, Jason에 관해 알 수 있는 내용이 <u>아닌</u> 것은?

> Jason lives in the Gullah community. His basket name is Sunday.

a. Jason is his official name.

b. He was born on Sunday.

c. His brother's basket name is Sunday, too.

d. He is usually called Sunday in his community.

Linking

3 본문의 빈칸에 들어갈 말로 가장 알맞은 것은?

a. Therefore

b. For example

c. In fact

d. On the other hand

Summary

4 본문의 단어를 이용하여 요약을 완성하시오.

> Different cultures have different _____ customs. For example, in the African-American Gullah community, babies are given two names: one is an official name and the other is a _____ name. In Malaysia, many people don't have _____ names. Instead, they add their father's name to their own name with the term "_____" or "_____." In Korea, siblings have a common _____ in their _____ names.

우리 조상의 이름 짓기

지식백과

우리 조상들은 원래 고유한 우리말로 된 이름을 지어 불렀다. 하지만 유교사상이 전파됨에 따라 관청, 벼슬, 고장 이름과 함께 이름도 한자로 지어 부르게 되었다. 자신의 이름 외에도 태어나면 처음으로 지어주는 이름인 아명이 있었다. 옛날에는 유아기에 사망률이 높았기 때문에 소똥이, 개똥이 같은 하찮은 이름을 지어주면 무병장수한다는 믿음이 있었다.

개똥아!

▶ 조선 시대 왕의 이름에 관한 동영상을 만나 보세요. ● Time 5' 39"

John Who?

Until the early years of the Middle Ages, most people in Europe lived in small farming villages. Everyone knew their neighbors, and there was little need for last names or surnames. As the population and the towns grew, however, record keeping became tricky. Suppose there were six Johns in the village. Then, how was the tax collector to make sure which ones had paid their taxes? So, people needed to find ways to tell apart people who shared the same first name.

Some people created surnames based on where they lived. If one lived toward the east, "Easter" was a perfect choice. If one lived near the crossing point of the river, "Ford" was chosen as the surname. Others created surnames based on their occupations. For example, someone who baked bread for a living called himself "Baker." A blacksmith took "Smith" for his last name.

Many surnames were taken from personal characteristics. If one had brown hair, "Brown" served as a good surname. If someone was very tall, "Long" was a perfect choice. "Bright" and "Smart" are also surnames based on personal characteristics. Finally, one easy way to create surnames was to add "son" to the father's name. So, "Williamson," "Johnson," and "Davidson" came into being.

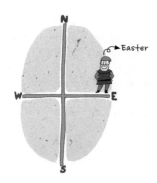

Words village 몡 마을   neighbor 몡 이웃   surname 몡 (이름의) 성   population 몡 인구   record 몡 기록
tricky 혱 힘든, 곤란한   suppose 동 가정하다   tax 몡 세금   collector 몡 수집가   toward 젼 …쪽으로
occupation 몡 직업   blacksmith 몡 대장장이   personal 혱 개인적인   characteristic 몡 특징

Main Idea

1 The main idea of the passage is _____.

a. why and how people got their surnames

b. what surnames were popular in the Middle Ages

c. how tax collectors used surnames to collect taxes

d. how surnames showed the relationships of family

Details

2 Why did people need to have last names?

a. People wanted to pay less tax.

b. More and more people lived in growing towns.

c. A lot of people liked to name their babies "John."

d. Everybody in the village knew all their neighbors.

Details

3 According to the passage, surnames were NOT based on _____.

a. where people lived

b. what people did for a living

c. what people looked like

d. how much people paid in taxes

Graphic Organizer

4 Complete the map with the words from the passage.

| Where does he _____? |
| e.g. Easter, Ford |

| What is his _____? |
| e.g. Baker, Smith |

What decides the surname for a man?

| Who is his _____? |
| e.g. Williamson, Johnson, Davidson |

| What are his _____ characteristics? |
| e.g. Brown, Long, Smart |

아이슬란드의 작명법

지식백과

30만 명의 인구를 가진 아이슬란드에서는 별도의 성을 사용하지 않으며 주로 아버지의 이름에 아들이면 'son'을 붙이고 딸의 경우는 'dottir'를 붙인 성을 사용한다. 1925년까지는 성을 만들 수 있었지만 그 이후에는 부모의 이름을 붙여 물려받을 수만 있게 되었다. 대부분 아버지의 이름을 사용하지만 어머니와의 관계를 표현하고 싶거나 아버지가 알 수 없는 사람의 경우 어머니의 이름을 사용하기도 한다.

Reading Closer 독해의 내공을 키우는 마무리 학습

A Unit 11에서 학습한 단어를 생각해 보고, 다음 퍼즐을 완성해 보시오.

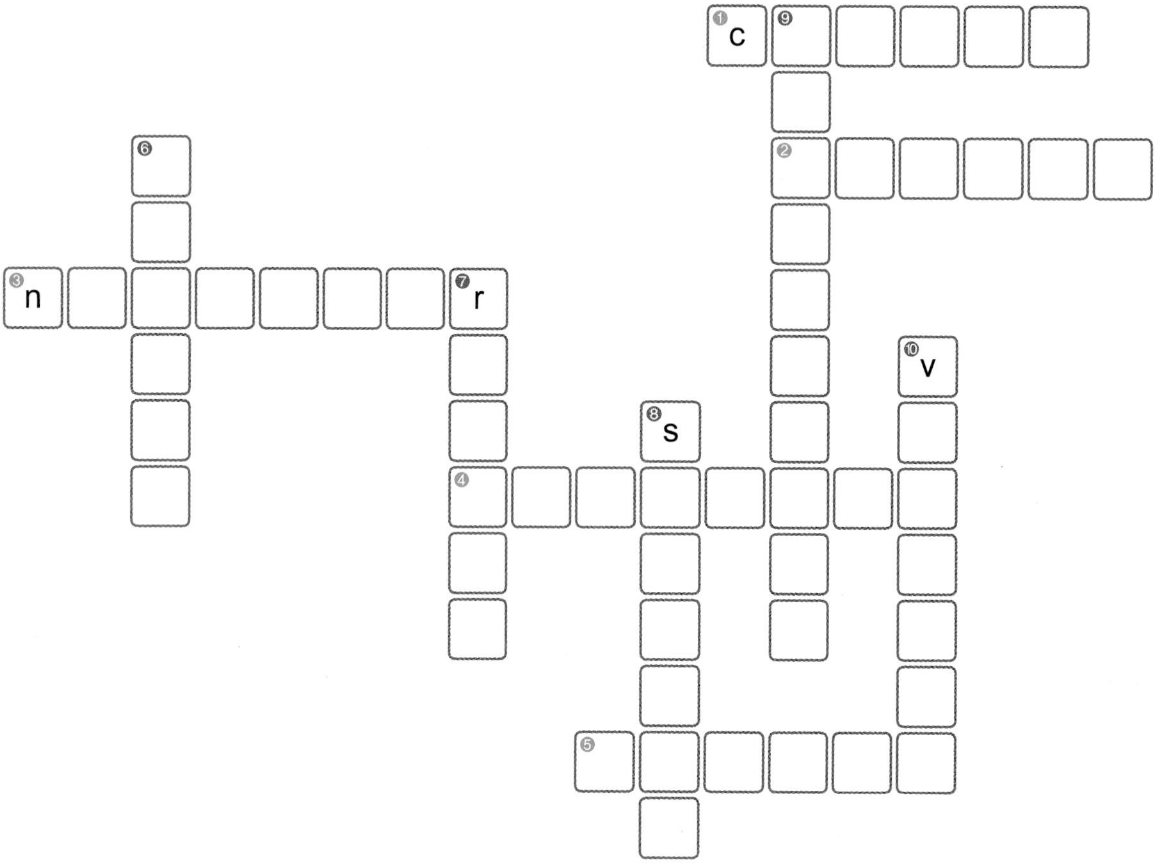

1 c
9
2
6
3 n
7 r
10 v
8 s
4
5

Across

❶ the opposite of rare or unusual

❷ 지방의 관습: a local __________

❸ a person who lives next to or near another person

❹ 공식 언어: __________ language

❺ very special or unusual

Down

❻ difficult to do or deal with

❼ 기록을 깨다: break the __________

❽ a brother or sister

❾ a similar word of job

❿ A __________ is a small town in the country.

B 다음 [보기]에서 알맞은 말을 골라 문장을 완성하시오.

보기   occupation   vary   consist   siblings   refer

1   Your ID should _____ of letters and numbers.

2   My mother studied at an art school and is an artist by _____.

3   The meaning of a smile can _____ from culture to culture.

4   He is the only child in his family, so he doesn't have any _____.

5   She always _____s to Ben as "that nice boy."

💡 생각을 키우는 서술형 • 수행평가 대비 훈련

C 다음 글을 읽고, 밑줄 친 부분 중 <u>어색한</u> 부분을 찾아 바르게 고치시오.

I come from Europe and have always been interested in names. My surname is Ford because, long ago, my family lived near a river. When I came to Korea, I tried to ⓐ<u>understand</u> Korean names. My friend's surname is "Kim," which means gold, so I asked, "Was someone in your family ⓑ<u>rich</u>?" I was thinking about names based on personal ⓒ<u>characteristics</u>. However, Korean surnames are not like that. The names aren't "Baker," "Brown," or "Long." Instead, Korea has ⓓ<u>the same</u> culture. In Korea, sibling's names sometimes ⓔ<u>share</u> a syllable. My friend Jun-seong has a brother, Jun-woo. How interesting!

_____ → _____

#*Topic* Painkiller, Aspirin & Placebo Effect

'낙타가 바늘구멍에 들어가기'란 속담은 엄청난 노력과 행운이 따르지 않고서는 이루어질 수 없는 일을 비유할 때 쓰여요. 우리가 아플 때 고통을 relieve하기 위해 먹는 약의 invention 과정을 이에 비유할 수 있어요. 물질의 발견부터 의약품의 허가까지 12~15년 정도의 기간과 약 10억 달러의 어마어마한 비용이 들어 간다고 해요.

인류가 초기에 만든 약의 주요 element는 우리에게 familiar한 자연에서 discover한 것들이었어요. 하지만 오늘날의 대부분의 약은 병에 유효한 성분들을 화학적으로 합성해서 만들어요. Painkiller인 아스피린도 화학적으로 합성하여 만든 약이에요. 이런 약들은 예기치 않게 우리 몸에 부작용을 일으키기도 해서 새로운 약을 개발할 때는 그 약이 가지고 있는 효과를 정확하게 demonstrate해야 해요. 그래서 임상 실험을 여러 단계를 걸쳐야만 하는데요. 우선 사람에게 시험하기 전 동물에게 먼저 약을 투여해서 effective한지 알아봐요. 이후 환자뿐만 아니라 건강한 사람에게도 시험을 해서 독성 여부나 몸의 흡수율을 조사해요. 실험 단계가 간단하지는 않겠죠? 이렇게 약을 개발하는 일은 참 어려운 일인데요. 이어지는 글을 통해 우리에게 친근한 약인 아스피린은 어떻게 개발되었는지 함께 알아봐요.

본문 미리보기 **QUIZ**

1 [☐ 버드나무 / ☐ 은행나무] 의 특정 성분은 통증을 완화 시킨다. 98쪽에서 확인

2 속임약 효과는 뇌의 [☐ 엔도르핀 / ☐ 아드레날린] 과 관련 있다. 100쪽에서 확인

☐ 1	**chemist** [kémist]	명 화학자	물리 화학자	physical _____
☐ 2	**claim** [kleim]	동 주장하다	강하게 주장하다	strongly _____
☐ 3	**compare** [kəmpéər]	동 비교하다	…와 비교하다	_____ to
☐ 4	**deceive** [disíːv]	동 속이다	대중을 속이다	_____ the public
☐ 5	**demonstrate** [démənstrèit]	동 입증하다	학설을 증명하다	_____ a theory
☐ 6	**discover** [diskʌ́vər]	동 발견하다	사실을 발견하다	_____ a fact
☐ 7	**effective** [iféktiv]	형 효과적인	효과적인 방법	an _____ method
☐ 8	**element** [éləmənt]	명 성분, 요소	중요 요소	a key _____
☐ 9	**ethical** [éθikəl]	형 윤리적인	윤리적인 문제	an _____ issue
☐ 10	**familiar** [fəmíljər]	형 친숙한, 익숙한	…에 익숙하다	be _____ with
☐ 11	**invention** [invénʃən]	명 발명	인쇄술의 발명	the _____ of printing
☐ 12	**painkiller** [péinkìlər]	명 진통제	진통제를 먹다	take a _____
☐ 13	**prescribe** [priskráib]	동 처방하다	약을 처방하다	_____ medicine
☐ 14	**relieve** [rilíːv]	동 덜어주다	스트레스를 풀다	_____ stress
☐ 15	**suffer** [sʌ́fər]	동 고통받다	통증으로 고생하다	_____ from pain

어휘 자신만만 QUIZ

1 아스피린은 고대로부터 중요한 진통제였다.

Aspirin has been an important _____ since ancient times.

2 그들은 의사들이 환자들을 속인다고 주장한다.

They _____ that doctors deceive the patients.

The Most Famous Painkiller

🕐 My Reading Time | Words 201 / 2분 10초

1회 _____ 분 _____ 초   2회 _____ 분 _____ 초

Aspirin has been an important painkiller since ancient times. The history of aspirin dates back to Hippocrates, the ancient Greek physician who lived sometime between 460 BC and 377 BC. He used powder from the bark and leaves of the willow tree to take care of headaches, pains, and fevers. By 1829,

5 chemists discovered that the element called salicin in willow plants helped relieve pain. People thought there would be no more pain for human beings.

But salicin from willow plants was tough on stomachs. In 1853, French scientist Charles Frederic Gerhardt found a way to solve the problem. However, his formula was difficult to make. In 1897, German chemist Felix Hoffmann

10 came up with a more efficient method and gave it to his father who was suffering from *arthritis. It successfully worked. The resulting compound received its familiar name of aspirin in 1899. Aspirin was sold as a powder before the first aspirin tablets were made in 1915.

The invention of aspirin soon led to its worldwide

15 spread in the 1920s. Throughout the 20th century, many uses for aspirin were found. Aspirin is now being used to reduce *swelling, ease heart problems, and relieve arthritis. Aspirin _____.

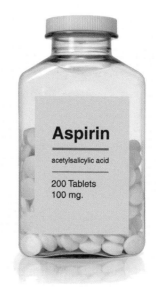

* **arthritis** 관절염
* **swelling** (살갗의) 부기

Words   painkiller 몡 진통제   history 몡 역사   bark 몡 나무껍질   willow 몡 버드나무   chemist 몡 화학자
   discover 통 발견하다   element 몡 성분, 요소   relieve 통 덜어주다   tough 혱 거친   formula 몡 제조법
method 몡 방법   suffer from …로 고통을 받다   compound 몡 혼합물   familiar 혱 친숙한, 익숙한

Main Idea

1 본문의 요지로 가장 알맞은 것은?

a. the side effect of salicin

b. the use of salicin as a painkiller

c. the oldest willow tree in the world

d. the invention of aspirin and its uses

Details

2 아스피린에 관한 설명 중 본문의 내용과 일치하지 <u>않는</u> 것은?

a. Aspirin was invented by a German chemist.

b. The name of aspirin was decided in 1899.

c. When aspirin was first sold, it was in liquid form.

d. Aspirin is used to ease heart problems.

Inference

3 빈칸에 들어갈 말로 가장 알맞은 것은?

a. is not often used as before

b. has become more than a painkiller

c. has been sold for about 100 years

d. is not being sold as a painkiller anymore

Summary

4 본문의 단어를 이용하여 요약을 완성하시오.

Aspirin has been used as a _____ for a long time. Hippocrates used powder from _____ plants to relieve pain, which was later found out to contain _____. Salicin was tough on _____. German chemist Felix Hoffmann made a formula to remove the side effect. In 1899, the compound got its present name, aspirin. Since the 20th century, aspirin has been widely used not only as a painkiller, but also for various diseases such as swelling, _____ problems, and arthritis.

지식백과

20세기 위대한 발견, 페니실린

페니실린은 곰팡이에서 얻은 화학 물질로 박테리아로 발생한 병을 치료하는 데 사용되는 항생제의 한 종류이다. 알렉산더 플레밍은 푸른곰팡이가 자라는 주변에는 박테리아가 자라지 못하는 것을 관찰하고 곰팡이가 박테리아를 자라지 못하게 하는 물질을 분비한다는 결론을 내렸다. 플레밍은 그 물질을 페니실린이라고 불렀다. 페니실린의 발견은 인류의 평균 수명을 높이고 항생 물질 연구의 출발점이 되었다.

▶ 건강한 삶을 가능하게 한 의약품의 발전에 관한 동영상을 만나 보세요. ⏱ Time 4' 08"

⏱ My Reading Time | Words 198 / 2분 11초

1회 ____ 분 ____ 초   2회 ____ 분 ____ 초

How do we know whether a new drug is effective? Usually, two groups of people take part in an experiment. One group is given the new drug, whereas the other group is given a placebo. A placebo is a pill that looks exactly the same as the new drug but is not real medicine. Later, the results from the two groups are compared to see _____.

Surprisingly, about one-third of people got better thanks to placebos. This is called the placebo effect. Some researchers believe that the effect comes from the mind. According to this theory, people's trust in a placebo helps them feel well and ultimately get better. Placebos may also bring about a physical response. One recent study demonstrated that the placebo effect is related to endorphins, the brain's own natural pain relievers.

Doctors have used placebos for ages. More than half of doctors in the U.S. regularly prescribe placebos, such as vitamins, to help their patients. Some people think that the practice is not ethical. They claim that doctors deceive the patients. Others, however, don't see anything wrong with doctors prescribing them. After all, these doctors are doing so to help their patients.

Words drug 명 약   effective 형 효과적인   take part in …에 참여하다   experiment 명 실험   placebo 명 속임약   result 명 결과   compare 통 비교하다   theory 명 이론   response 명 반응   demonstrate 통 입증하다   prescribe 통 처방하다   ethical 형 윤리적인   claim 통 주장하다   deceive 통 속이다

Title

1 Match each paragraph with an appropriate title.

(1) Paragraph 1 •   • a. How Do Doctors Use Placebos?

(2) Paragraph 2 •   • b. What Is the Placebo Effect?

(3) Paragraph 3 •   • c. What Is a Placebo?

Inference

2 Which best fits in the blank?

a. why the people prefer placebos

b. whether the new drug has been effective

c. how many people experienced the placebo effect

d. if the people found out that they were not given real medicine

Reference

3 Write what the underlined doing so refers to.

→ _____

Graphic Organizer

4 Complete the map with the words from the passage.

Placebo		
Definition	A pill that looks the _____ as medicine but is not _____ medicine	
Placebo Effect	• Some people get _____ with placebos. • _____ in a placebo helps patients get better. • It also causes a physical response, related to _____.	
Controversy	Some people think prescribing placebos is not _____, while others think it is OK.	

지식백과 노세보 효과 (Nocebo Effect)

속임약 효과와는 반대의 결과를 가져오는 것이 노세보 효과이다. 즉 병에 효과가 있는 약을 처방했음에도 불구하고 환자가 이를 믿지 않아 약효가 발휘되지 않거나 부작용이 있을 거라는 생각 때문에 건강을 해치는 결과로 이어지는 것을 말한다. 의사가 약물이나 시술의 부작용에 대해 지나치게 자세히 설명하는 것이 오히려 환자의 건강에 부정적인 효과를 가져올 수 있다는 비판이 제기되기도 한다.

A Unit 12에서 학습한 단어를 생각해 보고, 다음 퍼즐을 완성해 보시오.

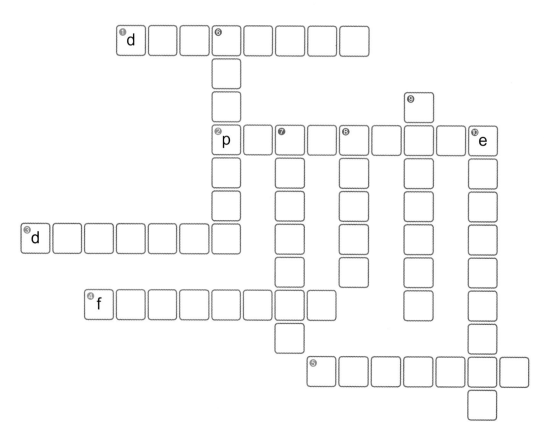

👉 **Across**

❶ to see, find, or become aware of something for the first time

❷ Doctors _____ medicine to their patients.

❸ to make someone believe something that is not true

❹ …에 익숙하다: be _____ with

❺ a similar word of reduce or remove

👇 **Down**

❻ to say that something is similar to something else

❼ 윤리적인 문제: an _____ issue

❽ 강하게 주장하다: strongly _____

❾ _____ is the study of past events.

❿ 효과적인 방법: an _____ method

B 다음 [보기]에서 알맞은 말을 골라 문장을 완성하시오.

> 보기 successfully   demonstrate   experiment   prescribed   relieve

1 The doctor _____ the medicine for my stomachache.

2 Tomorrow, she will _____ how the new software works.

3 To complete the course _____, you shouldn't skip the class.

4 This medicine will help you _____ your pain.

5 In the _____, participants were divided into two groups.

🔆 **생각을 키우는 서술형 · 수행평가 대비 훈련**

C 다음 [보기]에서 알맞은 말을 골라 글을 완성하시오.

> One time I took part in an _____. It was not a scientist who did the research; it was my mother! I said, "I don't feel well. I have _____ in my foot." She gave me a small, white pill. Several hours later, she asked me, "How do you feel now?" I felt better. "The pain in my foot is gone!" I said. My mother smiled. She told me the pill was not aspirin or other _____. It was candy, a _____. She said that _____ in my brain, not medicine, had made me feel better. We both laughed.

> 보기 placebo   medicine   pain   experiment   endorphins

#*Topic* Animated Cartoon & An Animation Festival

어른, 아이 할 것 없이 모두에게 사랑 받는 entertainment 인 만화 영화는 사실 영화보다 더 먼저 만들어졌어요. 1892년 프랑스에서 에밀 레노는 자신이 발명한 동화를 영사하는 장치로 소규모 극장에서 〈시각 극장〉을 열어 700여 개의 그림으로 구성된 움직이는 영상을 보여 줬어요. 그 이후 사진술이 접목되면서 만화 영화는 빠른 속도로 발전하게 돼요.

〈에밀 레노가 발명한 영사기〉

만화 영화를 만드는 원리는 사실 간단해요. 아마 여러분도 한 번쯤 해 본 적이 있을 거예요. 책의 한쪽 끝에 그림을 계속 그려서 휘리릭 넘기면 그림이 움직이는 것처럼 보이죠? 이것이 만화 영화의 원리예요. 여러 장의 still한 이미지의 sequence 를 연속적으로 보여 주어 마치 움직이는 것처럼 보이게 하는 것이죠. 그런데 lifelike한 움직이는 그림을 만들려면 1초당 24개의 separate된 그림을 그려야 해요. 그래서 한 편의 만화 영화를 만들기 위해서는 엄청난 수의 그림이 necessary하답니다.

처음 만들어진 이래로, 만화 영화는 많은 사람들에게 상상의 날개를 펼칠 수 있는 opportunity 를 제공해 왔어요. 이제 컴퓨터 기술의 발전과 함께 더 놀라운 이야기들을 우리에게 보여 주고 있죠. 신기한 만화 영화의 세계에 대해 다음 글에서 좀 더 자세히 알아볼까요?

본문 미리보기 QUIZ

1 만화 영화는 ▢ 19세기 초 / ▢ 20세기 초 에 처음 등장했다.

106쪽에서 확인

2 '하울의 움직이는 성'은 ▢ 미야자키 하야오 / ▢ 미셸 오실롯 의 작품이다.

108쪽에서 확인

☐ 1	**anniversary** [æ̀nəvə́ːrsəri]	명 기념일	결혼기념일	wedding ＿＿＿＿＿
☐ 2	**ashamed** [əʃéimd]	형 부끄러운	…을 부끄러워하다	be ＿＿＿＿＿ of
☐ 3	**celebrate** [séləbrèit]	동 축하하다	새해를 축하하다	＿＿＿＿＿ the New Year
☐ 4	**curse** [kəːrs]	동 저주하다	세상을 저주하다	＿＿＿＿＿ the world
☐ 5	**entertainment** [èntərtéinmənt]	명 오락물	가족 오락물	family ＿＿＿＿＿
☐ 6	**imprisoned** [impríznd]	형 수감된	수감된 범죄자	＿＿＿＿＿ criminal
☐ 7	**lifelike** [láiflaik]	형 실물과 똑같은	실물과 똑같은 조각상	a ＿＿＿＿＿ statue
☐ 8	**necessary** [nèsəséri]	형 필요한	필요한 경비	＿＿＿＿＿ expense
☐ 9	**opportunity** [àpərtjúːnəti]	명 기회	기회를 놓치다	lose an ＿＿＿＿＿
☐ 10	**passion** [pǽʃən]	명 열정	열정적인 사람	a man of ＿＿＿＿＿
☐ 11	**penniless** [pénilis]	형 매우 가난한	몹시 가난하게 되다	become ＿＿＿＿＿
☐ 12	**photograph** [fóutəgræf]	동 사진을 찍다	풍경을 찍다	＿＿＿＿＿ scenery
☐ 13	**separate** [sépərèit]	동 분리하다	빵을 분리하다	＿＿＿＿＿ the bread
☐ 14	**sequence** [síːkwəns]	명 연속된 한 장면	순서대로	in ＿＿＿＿＿
☐ 15	**still** [stil]	형 정지한	정지해 있다	stay ＿＿＿＿＿

어휘 자신만만 QUIZ

1 만화 영화가 정지한 이미지의 연속일 뿐이라는 것을 깨닫는 이는 거의 없다.

Few realize that an animated cartoon is only a series of ＿＿＿＿＿＿＿ images.

2 당신이 만화 영화를 사랑하는 사람이라면 이 기회를 놓치지 마세요.

Don't miss this ＿＿＿＿＿＿＿ if you are a cartoon lover.

Bring Images to Life

The animated cartoon first appeared in the early 20th century. Since then, many people have enjoyed this type of entertainment. Every year animated cartoons are big hits around the world. Movie-goers of all ages are fascinated by the excitement that animated cartoons offer.

5 　Few realize, however, that an animated cartoon is only a series of "still" images. The still images are shown at a very fast rate in a sequence. As many as 24 images are shown per second. Together, the images appear to be moving.

　A still image is called a frame. There are two main ways to make frames. In one way, images are drawn and then photographed to make frames. The other

10 way is to make use of a model frame. A model frame is made and changed in small ways. Then a special camera is used to photograph the results.

　An animated cartoon needs a huge number of frames, so it wasn't easy to produce a good one. Thanks to computer technology, however, it is now easier to create lifelike characters using special software. _____, skilled animators

15 are still necessary. After all, computers are not yet capable of making artistic choices and bringing real passion to simple images.

Words

animated cartoon 만화 영화　　entertainment 뎽 오락물　　excitement 뎽 흥분　　offer 뚕 제공하다
still 뼹 정지한　　sequence 뎽 연속된 한 장면　　photograph 뚕 사진을 찍다　　create 뚕 창조하다
lifelike 뼹 실물과 똑같은　　animator 뎽 만화 영화 제작자　　necessary 뼹 필요한　　passion 뎽 열정

Title

1 본문의 다른 제목으로 가장 알맞은 것은?

a. People's Love of Cartoons

b. Need for Skilled Animators

c. Basics of Animated Cartoons

d. The Early History of Animated Cartoons

Liking

2 빈칸에 들어갈 말로 가장 알맞은 것은?

a. Therefore

b. Nevertheless

c. Unfortunately

d. In other words

Details

3 본문의 내용에 관한 <u>두 가지</u> 질문을 고르시오.

a. How do still images appear to be moving?

b. Where are most animated cartoons made?

c. How are frames for animated cartoons produced?

d. What kind of software is good for making cartoons?

Summary

4 본문의 단어를 이용하여 만화 영화에 관한 표를 완성하시오.

Popularity
People love _____ cartoons.

Hidden Process
An animated cartoon is a series of _____ images shown very quickly.

Animated Cartoons

Two Ways to Make Frames
1. Images are drawn and _____.
2. A _____ frame is made and then changed in small ways.

Technology Help
Computer technology helps, but skilled _____ are still needed.

세계 최초의 만화 영화 제작자, 에밀 콜(Emile Cohl)

1857년 프랑스 파리에서 출생한 에밀 콜은 세계 최초로 만화 영화를 제작해 근대 만화 영화의 기틀을 마련한 창시자이다. 그는 수많은 작품을 남겼으며 후대의 유명한 영화감독들에게 영향을 끼쳤다. 그는 1908년 세계 최초의 만화 영화인 「판타스마고리」를 제작했다. 700장이 넘는 그림을 손수 그려 한 프레임씩 필름 카메라로 촬영하여 제작했다. 상영 시간은 1분 18초였다.

▶ 「판타스마고리」를 동영상으로 만나 보세요. ● Time 1' 16"

My Reading Time | Words 202 / 2분 12초

1회 _____ 분 _____ 초   2회 _____ 분 _____ 초

Candle Cinema is celebrating its thirtieth anniversary with cartoons from around the world. Four different cartoons are going to be shown on the same day. Don't miss this opportunity if you are a cartoon lover.

5

- **Date**: Sunday, October 7
- **Place**: Candle Cinema
- **Ticket Prices** Adult: $8, Kid under 12: $4
- **All day pass**
  Adult: $26 Kid under 12: $13

Movie Schedule
10:00 *Howl's Moving Castle*
12:15 *Azur & Asmar*
14:20 *The Man Who Planted Trees*
15:50 *Fantastic Planet*

Movie Reviews

10

Japan / Fantasy
Hayao Miyazaki
119min.

Sophie, a hatter, is cursed by the Witch of the Waste, and turns into an old woman. Ashamed of how she looks, she decides to run away. Along the way, she comes across Howl's moving castle. Inside the castle, Sophie meets the fire demon Calcifer whose work is making the castle move around. Calcifer promises to help her break the curse.

15

Azur & Asmar
Michel Ocelot

France / Adventure
Michel Ocelot
99min.

White-skinned, blue-eyed Azur and dark-skinned, brown-eyed Asmar are (A) rose / raised as brothers by Asmar's gentle mother. She tells them magical stories of the imprisoned Djinn Fairy (B) waiting / waited to be set free. One day Azur's father separates them. Azur is sent away to study, while Asmar and his mother are driven out, homeless and penniless. Years later, they meet again ...

20

Words

celebrate 통 축하하다   anniversary 명 기념일   opportunity 명 기회   hatter 명 모자 장수   curse 통 저주하다
ashamed 형 부끄러운   castle 명 성   promise 통 약속하다   imprisoned 형 수감된   set free 석방하다
separate 통 분리하다   penniless 형 매우 가난한   drive out 내쫓다

1 • Purpose

What is the purpose of the passage?

a. to promote an event

b. to recommend a movie

c. to compare animated cartoons

d. to announce ticket price changes

2 • Grammar

Choose the words that fit in boxes (A) and (B).

(A)	(B)		(A)	(B)
a. rose	⋯⋯ waiting		b. rose	⋯⋯ waited
c. raised	⋯⋯ waiting		d. raised	⋯⋯ waited

3 • Details

Write T if the statement is true and F if it is false.

(1) _____ Candle Cinema opened about thirty years ago.

(2) _____ Adults can see all four films with a $26 pass.

(3) _____ More than one animated movie will be shown before noon.

4 • Summary

Complete the summary with the words from the passage.

Candle Cinema is going to have an animation festival on Sunday, _____ 7. Tickets for each film are eight dollars, and an all day pass can be purchased for _____ dollars. Children under 12 get in for half price. Four movies will be shown: *Howl's Moving Castle*, *Azur & Asmar*, *The Man Who Planted Trees*, and _____ _____.

지식백과

애니메이션 축제의 시작, 안시 국제 애니메이션 축제

프랑스 남부의 작은 휴양 도시인 안시에서는 매년 6월 애니메이션 축제가 열린다. 일본, 캐나다, 크로아티아에서 열리는 애니메이션 축제와 함께 세계 4대 영화 애니메이션 축제로 꼽힌다. 상업 애니메이션뿐만 아니라 다양한 독립 단편 애니메이션이 함께 선보여 예술과 상업성을 적절히 조화시킨 행사로 평가받는다. 매년 20여만 명이 이 축제를 보기 위해 방문한다.

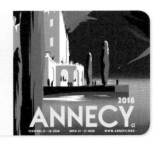

A Unit 13에서 학습한 단어를 생각해 보고, 다음 퍼즐을 완성해 보시오.

Across

❶ 다시 만날 것을 약속하다: _____ to meet again

❷ looking like a real person or thing

❸ 일자리를 제공하다: _____ a job

❹ to make or produce something

❺ not moving

❻ …을 부끄러워하다: be _____ of

Down

❶ 열정적인 사람: a man of _____

❼ to do something special or enjoyable for an important event, holiday

❽ so important that you must do it or have it

❾ the opposite of join or connect

B 다음 [보기]에서 알맞은 말을 골라 문장을 완성하시오.

보기	still	penniless	ashamed	raise	necessary

1 The child stood _____ without moving for several seconds.

2 It is _____ to eat fruits and vegetables every day.

3 He was jobless for some time and became _____.

4 The farmer decided to _____ more cows on the farm.

5 She was _____ that she had failed the important exam.

> 🔆 생각을 키우는 서술형 · 수행평가 대비 훈련

C 다음 글을 읽고, 밑줄 친 부분 중 틀린 부분을 찾아 바르게 고치시오.

> Jimin and Minsu ⓐare taking a class in computer animation. They are learning to produce still images ⓑcalled frames and put them in a sequence to make a story. They are enjoying their class a lot. Jimin's story is about a witch and a castle. It is not easy ⓒto make the witch to move through the castle. Jimin has to make many frames, but she is fascinated ⓓby producing animation. Minsu's story is about two children who ran away from home. He likes making artistic choices and ⓔusing the computer. Both Jimin and Minsu hope the class enjoy their short movies.

_____ → _____

생각의 폭을 넓히는 배경지식 Story

#Topic Nose, Snoring & Nose Hair

〈네페르티티의 흉상〉

세계 역사상 최고의 미인 중 한 명으로 꼽히는 네페르티티는 고대 이집트 왕의 아내였어요. 남겨진 조각상을 통해 그녀의 미모를 한눈에 알아볼 수 있는데요. 얼굴의 중심에 높지도 낮지도 않고 적당히 솟은 코와 이를 받치는 턱이 얼굴의 전체적인 균형을 maintain하고 있죠. 그래서 강인하고 지성적인 왕후의 특징이 잘 드러나고 있어요.

반면에 천재 화가 미켈란젤로는 낮고 못생긴 nasal 특징 덕분에 그의 작품 속에서 숨어 있는 그의 얼굴을 찾기 쉬운데요. 그는 아름다움에 대한 집착이 커서 수많은 걸작들이 탄생했다고 해도 과언이 아니라고 해요. 만약 그가 average한 코와 균형 잡힌 얼굴을 가졌다면 아름다운 걸작들이 존재했을까요?

〈미켈란젤로의 초상화〉

얼굴의 중심에 놓인 코는 외모적으로 뿐만 아니라 호흡 기관으로서 중요한 기능을 하는데요. 코는 우리가 breathe할 때 외부의 공기가 우리 몸속을 가장 먼저 지나가는 passage예요. 코 안의 코털은 마치 필터처럼 공기를 걸러 주고 코의 humidity를 유지해 주어 찬 공기가 바로 폐로 들어가는 것을 막아 줘요. 또한 후각 tissue는 냄새를 맡게 하죠. 이렇게 중요한 기능을 하는 코지만 잘 때 누군가 snore하는 소리로 잠을 설치게 하면 정말 괴로운 일이에요. 이어지는 글에서 코골이를 완화하는 방법에 대해 알아봐요.

본문 미리보기 QUIZ

1 코를 골 때 [☐ 베개를 베면 / ☐ 옆으로 자면] 코를 골지 않는 데 도움이 된다.

114쪽에서 확인

2 [☐ 코털은 / ☐ 후각 세포는] 공기 중의 세균, 먼지 등을 걸러 준다.

116쪽에서 확인

☐ 1	**attach** [ətǽtʃ]	통 붙이다	라벨을 붙이다	_____ a label
☐ 2	**average** [ǽvəridʒ]	명 평균	평균 수명	_____ life
☐ 3	**breathe** [briːð]	통 숨을 쉬다	숨을 들이쉬다	_____ in
☐ 4	**cautious** [kɔ́ːʃəs]	형 조심스러운	…에 대해 조심하는	_____ of
☐ 5	**clip** [klip]	통 (털, 잔가지를) 자르다	덤불을 자르다	_____ the bushes
☐ 6	**comfort** [kʌ́mfərt]	명 안락, 편안	안락하게 살다	live in _____
☐ 7	**humidity** [hjuːmídəti]	명 습도, 습기	높은 습도	high _____
☐ 8	**infection** [infékʃən]	명 감염	바이러스 감염	a virus _____
☐ 9	**maintain** [meintéin]	통 유지하다	질서를 유지하다	_____ order
☐ 10	**muscle** [mʌ́sl]	명 근육	근육의 힘	_____ power
☐ 11	**nasal** [néizəl]	형 코의	코 뼈	_____ bone
☐ 12	**passage** [pǽsidʒ]	명 통로	비밀 통로	a secret _____
☐ 13	**purpose** [pɔ́ːrpəs]	명 목적	인생의 목적	_____ of life
☐ 14	**snore** [snɔːr]	통 코를 골다	코를 크게 골다	_____ loudly
☐ 15	**tissue** [tíʃuː]	명 세포의 조직	지방 조직	fat _____

어휘 자신만만 QUIZ

1 사람들은 등을 대고 누워 잘 때 코를 곤다.

People _____ when they sleep on their backs.

2 습기는 호흡기 계통에 중요하다.

_____ is important for your respiratory system.

Reading

01

Home Remedy for Snoring

⏱ My Reading Time ｜ Words 214 / 2분 26초

1회 ____ 분 ____ 초　　**2회** ____ 분 ____ 초

Question

Sleepless How do I keep my roommate from snoring?

My roommate Jake is a good guy, but he snores like a motorbike. Every night I try to fall (A) | awake / asleep | before him. If I fail, I will have painful hours before I can sleep. What should I do?

Answers

5 　**Dr. Cureall** Tell him to sleep on his side, not on his back. Snoring is caused by vibrations in the tissues of his throat. When he sleeps on his back, the tissues in the throat slide back as the muscles relax. As air moves through the passage, the tissues vibrate, causing the snoring sounds.

　　Tball Dr. Cureall is right. People snore when they sleep on
10 　their backs. Here is a great way to keep your roommate from sleeping on his back. Cut a tennis ball in half and attach it to the back of his pajamas. When he lies on his back, it will give enough (B) | comfort / discomfort | to change his sleeping position. He will soon sleep on his side again.

15 　**Nasalstrip** Having him breathe through his nose is another way to help you out. A nasal strip will help him learn to breathe this way. The strips will open up his nose so more air comes in. Then he will stop breathing through his mouth.

Words

roommate 몡 룸메이트　　snore 통 코를 골다　　painful 혱 아픈　　cause 통 야기시키다　　vibration 몡 진동
tissue 몡 세포의 조직　　muscle 몡 근육　　passage 몡 통로　　attach 통 붙이다　　comfort 몡 안락, 편안
breathe 통 숨을 쉬다　　nasal 혱 코의　　strip 몡 가늘고 긴 조각

Topic

1 본문의 질문과 대답은 주로 무엇에 관한 것인지 고르시오.

a. sharing a room with a friend

b. keeping a person from snoring

c. breathing deeply through the nose

d. reducing physical pain

Details

2 다음 중 본문의 내용과 일치하지 <u>않은</u> 것은?

a. Jake snores terribly at night.

b. Sleepless is troubled by Jake's snoring.

c. Tball disagrees with Dr. Cureall's advice.

d. Nasalstrip thinks a nasal strip will be helpful.

Words

3 (A)와 (B)에 들어갈 말로 바르게 짝지어진 것은?

	(A)	(B)		(A)	(B)
a.	awake	comfort	b.	awake	discomfort
c.	asleep	comfort	d.	asleep	discomfort

Graphic Organizer

4 본문의 단어를 이용하여 코골이에 관한 표를 완성하시오.

Problem		Advice 1		Method
I can't sleep because of my roommate who _____.	➡	Have your roommate sleep on his _____.	⋯⋯	Attach a cut _____ _____ to your roommate's pajamas.

⬆ ⬇

Cause of Snoring		Advice 2		Method
The _____ of the throat _____		Have your roommate breathe through his _____.	⋯⋯	Use a _____ _____.

지식백과

수면 중에 호흡을 하지 않는다고?

코골이가 심한 사람들 중에는 수면 중에 호흡을 하지 않는 수면 무호흡증이 생긴다. 수면 중 최소 10초 이상 호흡을 멈추는 경우로 구강 내의 기도가 폐쇄되어 증상이 발생한다. 수면 중 호흡 정지가 빈번하게 일어나므로 잠을 자도 피로가 풀리지 않고 불면증으로 이어질 수 있다. 또한 저산소혈증으로 인한 다양한 심폐 혈관계의 합병증이 야기될 수 있다.

Don't Clip Your Nose Hair

Have you ever wondered why we have nose hair? It's definitely not for decoration or for the benefit of makers of nose hair trimmers. In fact, it plays an important role in keeping us healthy.

Nose hair works as a filter for our nasal passages. A person breathes in an average of 10,000 liters of air per day. When you breathe in air through your nose, you are breathing in the germs, fungus and dust in the air, too. Nose hair traps them. It keeps them from entering your lungs and (A) makes / making you sick.

Another purpose of nose hair is to maintain the humidity level of the nasal passages. It provides heat and moisture when you breathe in air and traps humidity when you breathe out. Humidity is important for your *respiratory system. Without nose hair, your throat would be dry and your lungs wouldn't work properly.

Overgrown nose hair may not be good to see, but it should never be removed completely. Without nose hair, you are more likely (B) getting / to get colds, allergy attacks and other infections. Older people should be cautious not to remove their nose hair because it often takes longer for clipped hairs to grow back.

* respiratory 호흡의

Words   trimmer 명 다듬는 기계   filter 명 여과 장치   nasal 형 코의   average 명 평균   germ 명 세균   fungus 명 곰팡이   lung 명 폐   purpose 명 목적   maintain 동 유지하다   humidity 명 습도   attack 명 공격   infection 명 감염   cautious 형 조심스러운   clip 동 (털을) 자르다

• Title

1 Another title for the passage could be " _____."

a. The Functions of Nose Hair

b. How to Remove Nose Hair

c. Nose Hair as a Decoration for Your Nose

d. Complexity of Our Respiratory Systems

• Grammar

2 **Choose the words that fit in boxes (A) and (B).**

	(A)	(B)		(A)	(B)
a.	makes	getting	b.	making	getting
c.	makes	to get	d.	making	to get

• Details

3 **Write T if the statement is true and F if it is false.**

(1) _____ Germs and dust come through our noses when we breathe out.

(2) _____ Nose hair helps our lungs work properly.

(3) _____ Nose hair prevents us from getting colds easily.

• Summary

4 **Complete the summary with the words from the passage.**

> Nose hair plays an important role in keeping us healthy. It works as a _____ for our nasal passages. It _____ germs, fungus and dust which come into our body when we _____ in air. Also, it helps maintain the _____ level of the nasal passages. So, it's not a good idea to remove nose hair. Nose hair keeps us from getting _____, allergy attacks and other infections easily.

지식 백과

우리 코의 기능

코는 들어오는 공기의 먼지를 정화하고 폐로 들어가기에 알맞은 온도와 습도가 되도록 해 준다. 코 천장의 후각점막은 공기 중에 섞여 들어오는 냄새를 맡게 하는 역할을 한다. 또한 성대에서 진동으로 만들어진 목소리를 코에서 더 울리게 하여 사람마다 다른 목소리의 차이를 만들어 낸다.

▶ 우리 코의 구조와 기능을 동영상으로 만나 보세요. ⏱ Time 3' 49"

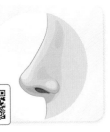

Reading Closer

독해의 내공을 키우는 마무리 학습

A

Unit 14에서 학습한 단어를 생각해 보고, 다음 퍼즐을 완성해 보시오.

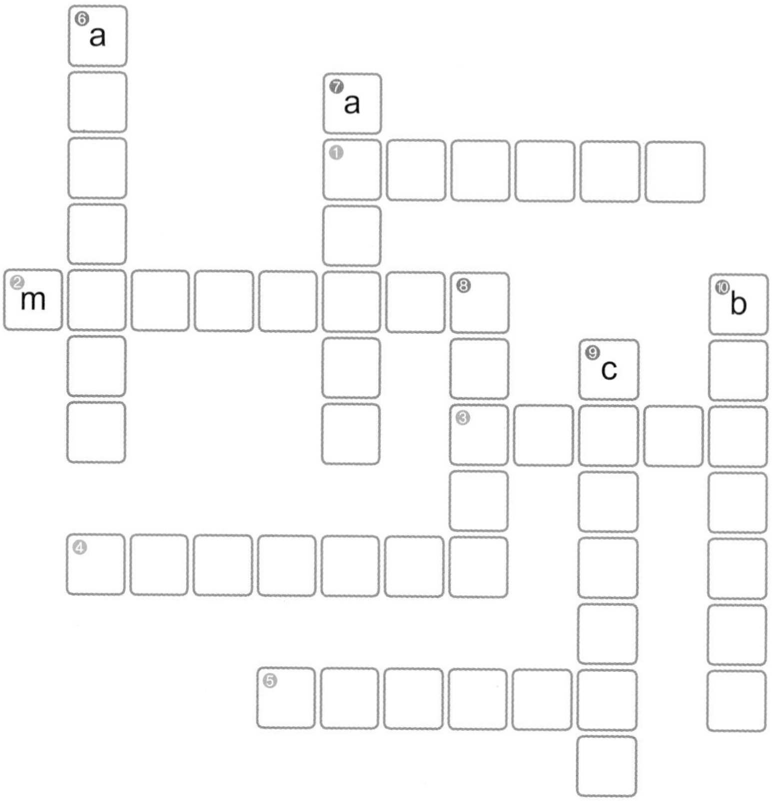

Across

① 지방 조직: fat __________

② 질서를 유지하다: __________ order

③ to breathe noisily while sleeping

④ causing pain to your body

⑤ to have interest in knowing or learning something

Down

⑥ 평균 수명: __________ life

⑦ the opposite of remove

⑧ 코 뼈: __________ bone

⑨ 안락하게 살다: live in __________

⑩ to move air into and out of your lungs

B 다음 [보기]에서 알맞은 말을 골라 문장을 완성하시오.

보기	asleep	attach	clip	vibration	prevent

1 I got the permission to _____ the poster on the wall.

2 CCTVs can help _____ and solve crimes.

3 The baby fell _____ while her dad sang a song.

4 You should put your cellphone on _____ mode during the meeting.

5 My father will _____ the bushes in the garden.

🔆 생각을 키우는 서술형 • 수행평가 대비 훈련

C 다음 글을 읽고, 밑줄 친 부분 중 어색한 부분을 찾아 바르게 고치시오.

My brother's snoring was keeping me up. Luckily, we ⓐsolved the problem. At first, I just asked him to sleep on his ⓑside, but then he changed his sleep position while sleeping. Then I asked him to ⓒattach a tennis ball cut in half to the back of his pajamas, but he said, "No. It will give me ⓓdiscomfort." Finally, we asked a doctor for help. The doctor said he should breathe through his ⓔmouth. "How?" we asked, and she showed us a special strip. "This will open your nasal passages and help you out," she said. It worked! Now we both sleep well.

→ _____ → _____

#*Topic* Bread, Prezel & Yeast

러시아에서는 결혼식 때 신랑의 어머니가 카라바이(karavay)라는 빵을 구워오는 풍습이 있다고 해요. 이 빵은 dough에 장식을 화려하게 해서 구워요. 신랑과 신부는 이 빵을 양쪽에서 한 입 크게 베어 무는데 더 크게 베어 문 사람이 결혼 생활의 주도권을 가지게 된다고 믿는데요. 재미있는 풍습인 것 같지 않나요?

우리가 보통 생각하는 빵은 도톰하게 rise한 모양이에요. 그런데 인류 최초의 빵은 밀가루 반죽을 그냥 불에 구워 납작한 모양으로 form했어요. 그렇다면 언제부터 이스트를 사용하여 부풀린 빵을 만들었을까요? 최초로 발효된 빵을 먹은 사람들은 고대의 이집트인이었어요. 그들이 어떻게 이스트를 발견하게 되었는지, 여러 가지 설이 있지만 분명한 것은 밀가루 반죽을 발효시켜 부풀려 먹었다는 것이에요. 실제로 이집트의 무덤에는 어떤 ingredient를 넣어서 어떻게 밀가루를 knead하는지에 관한 내용이 벽화로 남아 있어요. 또한 그들은 노동의 reward로 빵을 distribute했다고 해요.

그리스 로마 시대를 거쳐 제빵 기술이 본격적으로 발전해요. 기독교가 전파되며 제빵 기술도 유럽 각지로 퍼지면서 빵은 없어서는 안 되는 주식이 되었어요. 16세기의 빵은 사회적 지위를 나타내기도 했는데 흰 빵은 부를 상징하고, 갈색 빵은 가난을 상징했다고 해요. 알면 알수록 재미있는 빵에 대해 이어지는 글을 통해 좀 더 알아봐요!

본문 미리보기 QUIZ

1 끈 모양의 반죽을 꼬아서 만든 매듭과 고리 형태의 빵은 [☐ 프레츨 / ☐ 추로스] 이다. 122쪽에서 확인

2 [☐ 버터 / ☐ 이스트] 는 빵 반죽을 부풀게 하고 빵 맛을 부드럽게 한다. 124쪽에서 확인

독해의 장벽을 깨는 만만한 Vocabulary

Study Date: ____ / ____

☐ 1 **billion** [bíljən] 　형 십 억　　삼십 억년　　three _____ years

☐ 2 **chew** [tʃuː] 　동 씹다　　음식을 씹다　　_____ food

☐ 3 **distribute** [distríbjuːt] 　동 나누어 주다　　고르게 나누어 주다　　_____ evenly

☐ 4 **dough** [dou] 　명 밀가루 반죽　　밀가루 반죽을 만들다　　mix _____

☐ 5 **fold** [fould] 　동 접다　　옷을 접다　　_____ clothes

☐ 6 **form** [fɔːrm] 　동 만들어 내다　　새 낱말을 만들다　　_____ a new word

☐ 7 **ingredient** [ingríːdiənt] 　명 재료, 성분　　공통된 성분　　common _____

☐ 8 **knead** [niːd] 　동 주무르다　　밀가루를 반죽하다　　_____ flour

☐ 9 **knot** [nɑt] 　명 매듭　　매듭을 짓다　　tie a _____

☐ 10 **loop** [luːp] 　명 고리　　고리를 만들다　　make a _____

☐ 11 **multiply** [mʌltəplài] 　동 크게 증가하다　　열 배로 증가하다　　_____ ten times

☐ 12 **organism** [ɔ́ːrgənìzəm] 　명 유기체, 미생물　　유해한 미생물　　a harmful _____

☐ 13 **rise** [raiz] 　동 부풀다　　거품이 일다　　_____ in bubble

☐ 14 **reward** [riwɔ́ːrd] 　명 보상　　재정적인 보상　　a financial _____

☐ 15 **twist** [twist] 　동 비틀다　　실을 꼬다　　_____ thread

어휘 자신만만 QUIZ

1 이것은 긴 원통형의 밀가루 반죽으로 만들어 구운 음식의 일종이다.

It is a type of baked food made from long rolls of _____.

2 이것은 습기 찬 환경에서 당을 섭취하면 빠른 속도로 증식한다.

It _____ rapidly when it eats sugar in a moist environment.

Reading

01

The Oldest Snack Food

● My Reading Time | Words 193 / 2분 05초

1회 _____ 분 _____ 초   2회 _____ 분 _____ 초

A pretzel is a popular snack in Europe and North America. It is a type of baked food made from long rolls of dough. It has a unique shape: the knots and loops are made by twisting the strips of dough.

How did the first pretzel come into being? Nobody knows for sure. Many
5 people, however, say the pretzel is the oldest snack food ever developed. (A) According to some scientists, the pretzel was first developed in the early 7th century by a monk in southern France or northern Italy. (B) He formed the pretzel shape, which looked like a child's arms folded in prayer. (C) He used the pretzels as treats for kids who learned their prayers. (D) He called the snacks
10 "pretiola," which means "little reward" in Latin. In Italian, they were called "brachiola," which means "little arms."

The pretiolas found their way into Germany and Austria, where they became known as pretzels. Pretzels are said to have been brought over to America on the *Mayflower* in 1620. The pretzel market has grown in recent
15 years because pretzels are considered a healthy, fat-free snack.

Words

dough 몡 밀가루 반죽   unique 톙 독특한   knot 몡 매듭   loop 몡 고리   twist 통 비틀다   strip 몡 가느다란 조각
develop 통 발달하다   monk 몡 수도사   form 통 만들어 내다   fold 통 접다   prayer 몡 기도하는 사람
reward 몡 보상   consider 통 고려하다   fat-free 톙 무지방의

• Topic
1 본문의 다른 제목으로 가장 알맞은 것은?

a. The Unique Shape of Pretzels

b. A Short History of Pretzels

c. Different Names of Pretzels

d. The Growth of the Pretzel Market

• Organization
2 주어진 문장이 들어가기에 가장 알맞은 곳은?

> One day he had some dough left over after making bread.

a. (A) b. (B) c. (C) d. (D)

• Details
3 문장을 읽고 본문의 내용과 일치하면 T, 일치하지 않으면 F를 쓰시오.

(1) _____ Some people say pretzels were first made by a monk.

(2) _____ The Latin and Italian words for pretzels had the same meaning.

(3) _____ Pretzels got their present name in Germany and Austria.

• Graphic Organizer
4 본문의 단어를 이용하여 프레츨에 관한 표를 완성하시오.

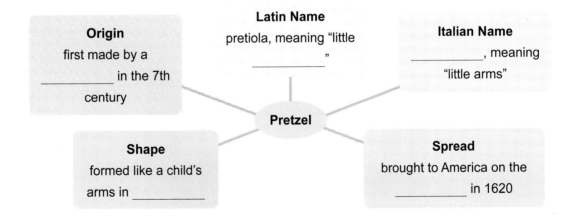

Origin
first made by a _____ in the 7th century

Latin Name
pretiola, meaning "little _____"

Italian Name
_____, meaning "little arms"

Pretzel

Shape
formed like a child's arms in _____

Spread
brought to America on the _____ in 1620

세계 여러 나라의 유명한 빵

지식 백과

프랑스의 빵으로 알려진 크루아상(croissant)은 초승달이라는 뜻으로, 헝가리에서 프랑스로 전해진 빵이다. 모양은 초승달 모양이다. 베이글(bagel)은 폴란드에 거주하던 유대인이 만든 빵으로, 독일어로 '반지 고리'라는 말에서 유래했다. 가운데 구멍이 뚫린 둥근 모양의 빵이다. 추로스(churros)는 반죽을 기름에 튀겨 낸 스페인 간식으로, 긴 막대 모양이다. churro라는 양의 뿔을 닮았다고 해서 붙여진 이름이다.

What Makes Bread Rise?

● My Reading Time | Words 209 / 2분 20초

1회 _____ 분 _____ 초 2회 _____ 분 _____ 초

How can simple ingredients like flour, sugar, salt, and eggs produce wonderfully bubbly bread? It is the work of the yeast, which creates soft, tasty bread. The bread dough rises because of the yeast in it. Without yeast, your bread would be too hard for you to even chew.

5　　Yeast, a kind of fungus, is a single-celled organism that can be seen only through a microscope. One gram of yeast contains 20 billion yeast cells! Though it is tiny, yeast is a living thing that can grow or die. It multiplies rapidly when it eats sugar in a moist environment. It dies when it is too cold or too hot. This is why _____ water is used to make bread dough.

10　　When you mix yeast with dough, the yeast starts to eat the sugar in the dough. As the yeast eats the sugar, it produces carbon dioxide and other chemicals. So, you can imagine that when dough becomes all bubbly inside, it puffs up.

Why does your mother knead the bread dough, then? It also has to do

15　with the yeast. Kneading the dough helps distribute the yeast cells evenly throughout the dough. This way, the dough rises evenly. Kneading also helps carbon dioxide bubbles form in the dough.

Words 　ingredient 몡 재료, 성분　flour 몡 밀가루　bubbly 혱 거품이 많은　yeast 몡 이스트　rise 동 부풀다　fungus 몡 곰팡이　single-celled 혱 단세포의　organism 몡 유기체, 미생물　microscope 몡 현미경　billion 혱 십 억의　multiply 동 크게 증가하다　environment 몡 환경　puff up 부어오르다　knead 동 주무르다　distribute 동 나누어 주다

1 • Main Idea

What is the main idea of the passage?

a. Yeast is the most important ingredient of bread.

b. Yeast mixes well with dough in a dry environment.

c. Yeast helps make soft bread by forming bubbles in the dough.

d. Yeast is a single-celled organism that cannot live in extreme cold.

2 • Inference

Which is the best choice for the blank?

a. cold   b. hot   c. warm   d. clean

3 • Details

Which question CANNOT be answered based on the passage?

a. What makes bread dough rise?

b. When does yeast die or multiply?

c. What does yeast produce when it eats sugar?

d. How many bubbles does a single yeast cell make?

4 • Summary

Complete the summary with the words from the passage.

Yeast helps make soft, tasty _____. Yeast is a single-celled _____ that grows well in _____ conditions. When it eats sugar, it produces _____ _____, which creates bubbles in the dough. _____ the dough does two things. First, it helps spread the yeast to every part of the _____. Second, it helps form _____ in the dough.

지식백과

이스트의 다양한 쓰임

yeast는 그리스어로 '끓는다'는 뜻으로, 이스트가 발효 중에 이산화탄소를 만들어 거품이 많이 생기는 것에서 유래했다. 이스트는 빵뿐만 아니라 맥주나 포도주의 제조에도 쓰이고 다양한 종류의 발효식품을 만드는 데도 빠질 수 없는 중요한 역할을 한다. 또한 이스트는 지방, 단백질 등 영양 성분을 포함하고 있어 사료로도 사용되고, 비타민 B군과 비타민 D를 함유하고 있어 의약품 공업에도 사용된다.

▶ 이스트의 발효 과정을 실험 동영상으로 만나 보세요. ● Time 4' 19"

Reading Closer 독해의 내공을 키우는 마무리 학습

A Unit 15에서 학습한 단어를 생각해 보고, 다음 퍼즐을 완성해 보시오.

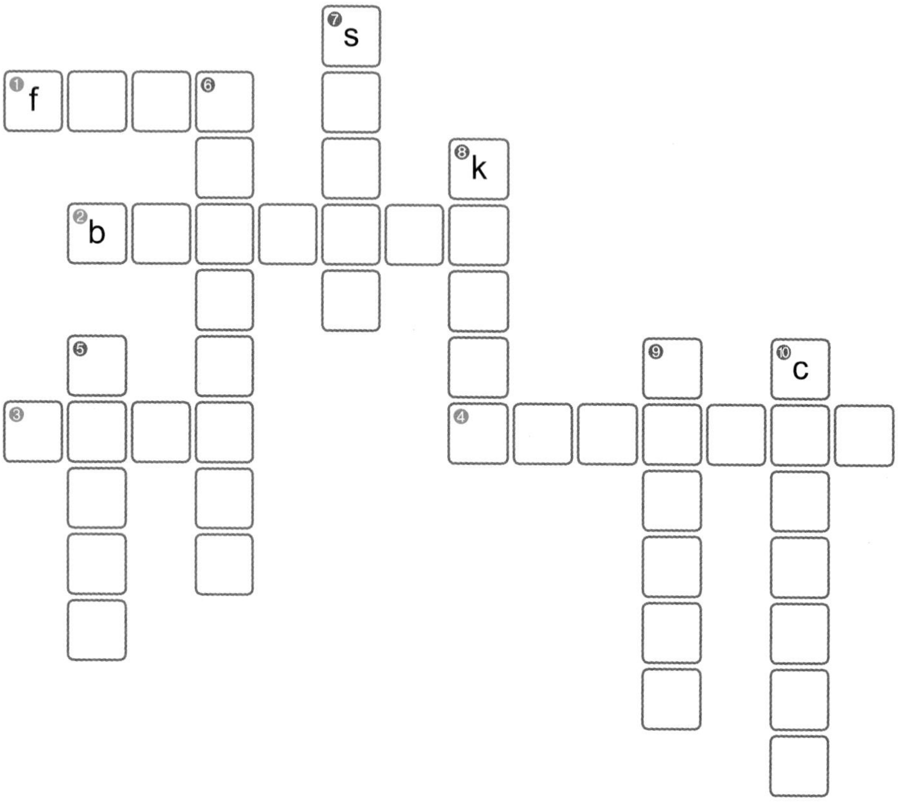

Across

❶ to cause something to have a particular shape

❷ 삼십 억년: three __________ years

❸ 고리를 만들다: make a __________

❹ 제품을 개발하다: __________ a product

Down

❺ A __________ is a mixture of flour, water, and other ingredients.

❻ to increase greatly in number or amount

❼ A __________ is a long, narrow piece of something.

❽ 밀가루를 반죽하다: __________ flour

❾ 보상을 받다: receive a __________

❿ to have something inside

B 다음 [보기]에서 알맞은 말을 골라 문장을 완성하시오.

| 보기 | reward | multiply | distribute | throughout | ingredient |

1 The typhoon caused serious damage _____ the nation.

2 He volunteered to _____ food to senior citizens in need.

3 Her parents bought her a bike as a _____ for her effort.

4 Germs can easily _____ inside a humidifier.

5 Mozzarella cheese is a major _____ of pizza.

생각을 키우는 서술형・수행평가 대비 훈련

C 다음 [보기]에서 알맞은 말을 골라 글을 완성하시오.

Last week, Kevin and Daniel made pretzels. They wanted to make a healthy, fat-free snack to share with their friends. They used simple _____, like flour, water, and salt. Of course, they also used a few grams of _____ to make the _____ rise. After mixing all the ingredients and kneading the dough, they made long rolls. Kevin wanted to twist the rolls into interesting _____. Daniel wanted to make the unique pretzel shape which looks like _____ arms. In the end, they made both shapes. The pretzels were very popular with their friends at school!

| 보기 | dough | ingredients | folded | yeast | knots |

#*Topic* Princess, Beautiful Song & Crystal

'A long time ago...'라는 말이 시작되면 모두가 재미있는 이야기에 대한 anticipation이 한껏 부풀어 오르죠. 이런 이야기들은 주로 사람들의 입에서 입으로 전해 내려오는 전래 동화예요. 이것은 재미뿐만 아니라 착하고 humble한 사람은 복을 받고 나쁜 사람들은 벌을 받는다는 권선징악(勸善懲惡)의 교훈을 줘서 사람들에게 오랫동안 beloved되어 오고 있어요.

전래 동화는 나라마다 각자의 문화가 잘 반영되어 있는데요. 신기하게도 서로 닮아 있는 이야기들도 많아요. 그중에서 「해와 달이 된 오누이」는 nearby한 동북아시아에도 널리 퍼져있는데요. 이야기에서 쫓고 쫓기는 관계가 다양하게 나타나요. 일본의 경우, 쫓는 것은 악마이고 아이들은 하늘로 올라가 별이 되었다고 해요. 중국의 이야기는 늑대가 하늘에서 떨어져 dead한 곳에 배추가 나와 아이들이 배추를 팔아 부자가 되었다고 해요. 이처럼 문화별로 비슷한 이야기가 있다는 것이 참 신기한데요. 사실 이런 전래 동화는 신화나 민담의 내용들이 어린이에게 알맞은 내용으로 바뀐 것이어서 원작은 우리가 아는 내용과 다르게 cruelty를 담고 있는 무서운 이야기도 있다고 해요.

자, 동심(童心)의 마음으로 동화 한 편을 읽어 보는 시간이에요. 이어지는 이야기는 베트남의 전래 동화랍니다. 이야기에 등장하는 공주가 무엇 때문에 슬퍼하고 있는지 함께 읽어봐요.

본문 미리보기 QUIZ

1 공주가 반한 아름다운 노래를 부른 사람은 [☐ 농부 / ☐ 어부] 였다.　　130쪽에서 확인

2 왕이 발견하여 찻잔으로 만든 것은 [☐ 수정 / ☐ 금] 이다.　　132쪽에서 확인

☐ 1	**anticipation** [æntìsəpéiʃən]	몡 기대	큰 기대를 갖고	with great _____
☐ 2	**beloved** [bilʌvd]	혱 사랑하는	나의 사랑하는 딸	my _____ daughter
☐ 3	**burst** [bəːrst]	됭 터지다	풍선을 터트리다	_____ the balloon
☐ 4	**cruelty** [krúːəlti]	몡 잔인함	잔인함을 보이다	show _____
☐ 5	**embroider** [imbrɔ́idər]	됭 수를 놓다	…에 수를 놓다	_____ on
☐ 6	**fisherman** [fíʃərmən]	몡 어부	어부의 아들	son of a _____
☐ 7	**fling** [fliŋ]	됭 내던지다	돌을 던지다	_____ a stone
☐ 8	**humble** [hʌ́mbl]	혱 겸손한, 초라한	겸손한 사람	a _____ person
☐ 9	**hut** [hʌt]	몡 오두막	통나무 오두막	a wooden _____
☐ 10	**nearby** [níərbái]	혱 가까운 곳의	가까운 도시	a _____ town
☐ 11	**pale** [peil]	혱 창백한	창백해지다	turn _____
☐ 12	**pour** [pɔːr]	됭 (음료를) 따르다	커피를 따르다	_____ coffee
☐ 13	**speechless** [spíːtʃlis]	혱 말을 못하는	말문이 막히다	be _____
☐ 14	**surface** [sə́ːrfis]	몡 표면	표면상으로	on the _____
☐ 15	**wound** [wuːnd]	됭 상처를 입히다	심하게 다치다	be seriously _____ed

어휘 자신만만 QUIZ

1 우리는 근처 마을에서 어부를 데려왔다.

We brought a fisherman from a _____ village.

2 그녀는 차의 표면에 어부의 얼굴을 보았다.

She saw the fisherman's face on the _____ of the tea.

A long time ago, there lived a king and his daughter. The princess spent most of her time in her room at the top of the tower, reading or embroidering.

One day, as the princess was sitting by the window, she heard a song from a fishing boat in the river.

5 "How beautiful the song is! The man who can sing such a beautiful song must be young and handsome."

From that day on, the princess waited by the window to hear the song again. But she could not hear it. As time went by, her anticipation changed into a broken heart. She became pale and weak.

10 Worried about his beloved daughter, the king spoke with the maid.

"My Lord, the princess is sick with love. You must find the handsome young man who sang this song," said the maid, and sang it. The king sent out his men at once.

A few days later, the men returned. "We brought a fisherman from a 15 nearby village. He can sing the song."

Seeing the fisherman, the king was _____. The fisherman was neither young nor handsome. How could he be the princess's husband?

The fisherman was brought to the princess's room and sang the song. As soon as she heard the song, the princess jumped from her bed and got dressed. She flung open the door.

Words   daughter 명 딸   embroider 동 수를 놓다   anticipation 명 기대   pale 형 창백한   beloved 형 사랑하는   maid 명 하녀   at once 즉시   return 동 돌아오다   fisherman 명 어부   nearby 형 가까운 곳의   speechless 형 말을 못하는   neither A nor B A도 B도 아닌   fling 동 내던지다

1 • Details

문장을 읽고 본문의 내용과 일치하면 **T**, 일치하지 않으면 **F**를 쓰시오.

(1) _____ The princess became sick because she didn't hear the song again.

(2) _____ The maid advised the king to find the man who sang the song.

(3) _____ The king wanted the fisherman to be the princess's husband.

2 • Grammar

본문에 밑줄 친 **must**와 의미가 같은 것은?

a. All students <u>must</u> keep quiet in the classroom.

b. He <u>must</u> be at home. I saw his car outside his garage.

c. I <u>must</u> go to the bank and get some money.

d. We <u>must</u> get together soon for lunch.

3 • Inference

본문의 빈칸에 들어갈 말로 가장 알맞은 것은?

a. satisfied   b. excited

c. speechless   d. frightened

4 • Prediction

어떤 일이 벌어질까요? 하나를 골라 자신의 예측을 쓰시오.

☐ The princess fell in love with the fisherman.

_____

_____

_____

☐ The princess was disappointed by the fisherman's appearance.

_____

_____

_____

지식백과

목소리의 힘, 메라비언의 법칙

한 사람이 상대방으로부터 받는 이미지는 시각적 요소가 55%, 청각적 요소가 38%, 말의 내용이 7%를 차지한다고 한다. 대화의 내용보다 시각·청각적 요소와 같은 비언어적인 부분이 93%에 해당한다. 같은 내용이라도 부드럽고 따뜻하며 신뢰감을 주는 목소리로 말하는 것이 상대방의 호감을 이끌어 낼 수 있다는 의미이다.

▶ 메라비언의 법칙에 대해 동영상으로 만나 보세요. ● Time 4' 07"

A Crystal Heart · **131**

The princess burst out laughing. Instead of a young and handsome prince, there stood a humble-looking fisherman. She turned her head away and said, "Close the door."

The fisherman was sent home. But he could hardly eat or sleep. He had
5 fallen in love. He grew ill. In a few days, the villagers found him dead in his hut. On his chest sat a large crystal.

"ⓐ It is his heart," the wise old woman in the village said. "The princess wounded him so deeply, his heart turned hard to stop the pain."

The villagers put ⓑ the crystal in the fisherman's boat and pushed ⓒ it to
10 the river. The boat came to the shore by the palace. The king found the crystal. He took ⓓ it to the palace and made it into a teacup. Then he gave it to his daughter.

That night, the princess poured tea into the cup and sat by the window. Just as she was about to drink, she saw the fisherman's face on the surface of
15 the tea. Her room filled with his sweet song. She remembered her own cruelty. "What have I done? I'm so sorry." Her tears dropped into the cup.

Words   burst 통 터지다   instead of … 대신에   humble 형 겸손한, 초라한   hardly 부 거의 …않다   ill 형 아픈
hut 명 오두막   crystal 명 수정   wound 통 상처를 입히다   pain 명 고통   shore 명 기슭, 해안가
palace 명 궁전   pour 통 (음료를) 따르다   surface 명 표면   cruelty 명 잔인함

Reference

1 Among ⓐ~ⓓ, which refers to something different?

   a. ⓐ   b. ⓑ   c. ⓒ   d. ⓓ

Changing Feelings

2 How did the princess's feelings change?

   a. surprised → satisfied   b. scornful → regretful

   c. sad → pleased   d. disappointed → terrified

Details

3 Which is true according to the story?

   a. The fisherman was young and handsome.

   b. A large crystal was found in the fisherman's hut.

   c. The wise old woman brought the crystal to the king.

   d. The princess felt happy to hear the fisherman's sweet song again.

Summary

4 Complete the summary with the words in the story.

> When a princess heard a beautiful song, she thought the singer must be young and _____. Actually, the singer was a humble-looking _____. The princess laughed at the man when she saw him. He, however, fell in _____ with her, became ill, and finally died. A large _____ was found on his chest. The king made a _____ from the crystal and gave it to the princess. When the princess poured tea into the cup, she heard his sweet _____. Then she remembered her own _____.

마음의 병, 상사병

지식백과

상사병이라는 말이 처음 사용된 것은 중국 송나라 때부터라고 한다. 송나라의 왕은 시종의 아내를 빼앗고 그 종은 멀리 귀양을 보냈는데, 서로를 몹시 그리워한 이 두 사람은 죽음을 택하게 된다. 이들의 무덤에서 각각 나무 한 그루가 자라났는데, 두 나무가 가지를 뻗어 다가가려고 하는 모습이 서로를 그리워하는 모습과 같다고 하여 상사수(相思樹)라고 부른 것에서 상사병이라는 말이 생겼다고 한다.

Reading Closer

독해의 내공을 키우는 **마무리 학습**

A   Unit 16에서 학습한 단어를 생각해 보고, 다음 퍼즐을 완성해 보시오.

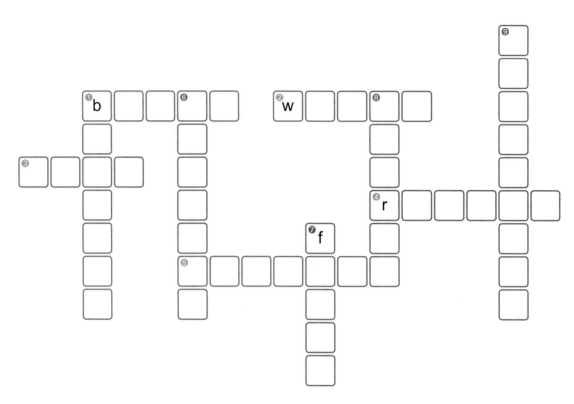

👉 **Across**

❶ to break open or into pieces in a sudden and violent way

❷ to injure someone or something by cutting or breaking the skin

❸ 창백해지다: turn _____

❹ the opposite of leave

❺ 잔인함을 보이다: show _____

👇 **Down**

❶ 내 사랑하는 딸: my _____ daughter

❻ 표면상으로: on the _____

❼ to throw or push something in a sudden and forceful way

❽ a similar word of close

❾ A _____ is a person who catches fish.

B 다음 [보기]에서 알맞은 말을 골라 문장을 완성하시오.

보기   cruelty   hardly   fling   surface   embroider

1   Tourists often _____ coins into Rome's Trevi Fountain.

2   About 70% of the Earth's _____ is covered with water.

3   She wants to _____ tiny flowers on the baby's scarf.

4   We often see scenes of _____ and violence from movie screens.

5   He felt so ashamed that he could _____ say a word.

🔅 생각을 키우는 서술형 · 수행평가 대비 훈련

C 다음 [보기]에서 알맞은 말을 골라 글을 완성하시오.

     Once there was a princess. She lived in a _____ with her maid. The princess had a very beautiful voice. One day, she sang a sad, sweet song at the window. Just then, a handsome young _____ was walking by. He heard the song and fell in _____. "But how can I love a princess? I am only a _____ man," he thought. But he had an idea. He made delicious tea for the _____. He gave it to the maid. When the princess took the tea, her face filled with love. "I had a dream. My husband made me tea. Where is he?"

보기   princess   humble   villager   palace   love

Make Your Own Quotes ✏️

앞에서 배운 내용 중에서
마음속에 간직하고 싶은
좋은 문장들을 여기에 적어 봅시다!

Remember what people used to say about flying in the air.
They said, "It's impossible! Only birds fly!" (76쪽)

사람들이 하늘을 나는 것에 대해 무엇이라고 이야기하곤 했는지를 기억하라. "그것은 불가능해! 새들만이 날 수 있어!"라고 이야기했다.

영어 1등급 STARTER

우리가 찾던 책이
바로 이거야

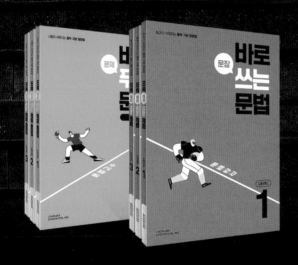

내가 쓰는 문장이
바로 내신의 평가문항이 되고

내가 읽는 지문이
바로 수능의 배경지식이 되고

바로 쓰는 문법 [기본]

- ▶ 2단계에 걸친 개념 반복 학습으로 문법 마스터
- ▶ 15개정 13종 교과서에서 뽑은 문장 쓰기 훈련
- ▶ 별책 부록으로 '핵심 개념노트(미니 개념북)' 증정

바로 읽는 배경지식 독해 [기본]

- ▶ 수능 배경지식 쌓고 독해력 키우는 기본 독해서
- ▶ 우리말 스토리&유튜브 영상으로 오래 기억하는 배경지식
- ▶ 재미있는 단어 퍼즐, 문장 끊어 읽기 등을 통한 독해 훈련

바로 푸는 문법 N제 [실전]

- ▶ 오답률 기반의 단계별 선택형/서술형 문제풀이 훈련
- ▶ 〈바로 쓰는 문법〉과 동일한 목차로 병행 또는 순차적 사용 가능
- ▶ 별책 부록으로 '내가 왜 틀렸을까(오답 노트)' 증정

바로 읽는 구문 독해 [실력]

- ▶ 급격히 어려워지는 고교 영어 내신 대비서
- ▶ 문장 구조 파악과 바른 해석을 훈련하는 독해서
- ▶ 구문 설명 → 문장 연습 → 독해 훈련으로 단계화

바로
읽는
독해

배경
지식

바로 읽는 독해

배경
지식

LEVEL
3

WORKBOOK

CHUNJAE
EDUCATION, INC.

바로 읽는 독해

WORKBOOK

바로 읽는 배경지식 독해

실력향상 WORKBOOK

LEVEL 3

01 Orange Marilyn

쉬운 독해를 위한 Vocabulary 업그레이드

A 다음 영어 표현을 읽고 뜻을 쓰시오.

1 expensive _____

2 appear _____

3 photograph _____

4 add _____

5 million _____

6 comment _____

7 object _____

8 modern _____

9 society _____

10 product _____

11 understand _____

12 recognize _____

13 price _____

14 original _____

15 famous _____

16 explain _____

B 다음 주어진 표현을 배열하여 우리말을 영어로 쓰시오.

1 왜 그의 작품이 그렇게 비쌀까? (expensive / is / his / so / art / why)

2 한 가지 이유는 그의 작품이 이해하기 어렵지 않다는 것이다.

(to understand / one / is / his / is not / reason / that / hard / work)

3 그 작품의 최초 가격은 비싸지 않았다.

(expensive / the original / was / the work / not / of / price)

4 그것은 레오 카스텔리에게 250달러에 팔렸다. (was / $250 / it / sold / Leo Castelli / for / to)

C

끊어 읽기 구문 학습으로 독해 실력 업그레이드

다음과 같이 끊어진 표시에 유의하여 읽고, 문장을 우리말로 해석하시오.

1   "Orange Marilyn" / is / a 20-by-16 inch silkscreen work / by Andy Warhol.

2   This style of art / starts / with a photograph. // The artist / then adds / colors / to change / the feeling / in the photo.

3   Some people / say / that / Warhol / was making / a comment / about a famous person / in this picture.

4   He / was saying / that, / in modern society, / a famous person / seems more like / a product / than a person.

5   Warhol / made / several silkscreens / showing / Marilyn Monroe. // The one / called / "Orange Marilyn" / is / the most famous.

6   When / "Orange Marilyn" / appeared / at auction / in 1998, / after / Warhol / had died, / however, / it / was sold / for $17.3 million.

7   The price / was / over 10,000 times / the amount / that / Castelli / had paid.

8   Through the years, / Warhol's works / have been sold / for more money / than Picasso's.

9   "With Warhol / you / don't have to explain / anything."

UNIT 01

02 The Life of Andy Warhol

쉬운 독해를 위한 Vocabulary 업그레이드

A 다음 영어 표현을 읽고 뜻을 쓰시오.

1	achieve	_____	9	employ	_____
2	advertising	_____	10	immigrant	_____
3	celebrity	_____	11	illustrator	_____
4	commercial	_____	12	suggest	_____
5	elevate	_____	13	found	_____
6	successful	_____	14	mass-produce	_____
7	graduation	_____	15	different	_____
8	remove	_____	16	position	_____

B 다음 주어진 표현을 배열하여 우리말을 영어로 쓰시오.

1 그는 곧 성공적인 삽화가가 되었다. (illustrator / he / became / a successful / soon)

2 일상의 사물을 그린다는 생각은 그의 친구 중 한 명으로부터 나온 것이었다.

(painting / came from / his friends / one of / daily objects / of / the idea)

3 그는 어린 나이일 때부터 스케치와 그림에 재능을 보였다.

(an early age / a talent / painting / at / and / showed / he / drawing / for)

4 그는 이 위치를 힘들게 노력해서 얻었다. (hard work / he / position / through / achieved / this)

끊어 읽기 구문 학습으로 독해 실력 업그레이드

C 다음과 같이 끊어진 표시에 유의하여 읽고, 문장을 우리말로 해석하시오.

1   Andy Warhol / was born / in 1928 / in Pittsburgh / as a son of / Slovak immigrants.

2   He / studied / commercial art / at the Carnegie Institute of Technology.

3   After graduation, / he / went to / New York / and / worked / as an illustrator / for magazines / and commercial advertising.

4   In the 1960s, / Andy Warhol / started painting / daily objects / such as Campbell Soup cans / and Coke bottles.

5   He / suggested / Andy / should paint / the things / he / loved / most.

6   He / made / silkscreen prints / of famous people / like Marilyn Monroe / and Elizabeth Taylor.

7   He / employed / "art workers" / and / mass-produced / his silkscreen prints / with different versions.

8   He / was / the artist / who / elevated / subjects of everyday life / to the level of art.

9   He / was / also the one / who / removed / the difference / between / fine art / and / commercial art.

01 Animals and Memory

쉬운 독해를 위한 Vocabulary 업그레이드

A 다음 영어 표현을 읽고 뜻을 쓰시오.

1 difference _____

2 memory _____

3 remember _____

4 event _____

5 short-term _____

6 forget _____

7 last _____

8 survive _____

9 connect _____

10 create _____

11 history _____

12 past _____

13 recent _____

14 research _____

15 allow _____

16 happen _____

B 다음 주어진 표현을 배열하여 우리말을 영어로 쓰시오.

1 인간의 기억과 개의 기억 사이에는 큰 차이가 있다.

(between / a dog's / there / and / difference / a person's memory / a big / is)

2 당신은 심지어 입었던 옷도 기억을 할지 모른다.

(even / wearing / you / were / what / may / remember / you)

3 개들은 사건이 일어난 후 2분이 지나면 그 사건을 잊어버릴 수 있다.

(forget / happens / dogs / an event / after / it / may / two minutes)

4 동물들은 자신들이 생존하도록 도와주는 것들을 기억한다.

(help / animals / which / them / survive / remember / things)

끊어 읽기 구문 학습으로 독해 실력 업그레이드

C 다음과 같이 끊어진 표시에 유의하여 읽고, 문장을 우리말로 해석하시오.

1 When / you / meet / an old friend, / you / remember / where and when / you / last met.

2 In other words, / you / remember / an event. // Recent research / indicates / that / animals / cannot do / this.

3 In fact, / it / seems / that / many animals / have / terrible short-term memories.

4 Many animals, / from dolphins / to bees, / have / memories / which / only last / seconds.

5 "But wait," / you / might say. // "What about / the saying / 'an elephant / never forgets' / and things like that?

6 For instance, / some birds / remember / where / they / left / their food. // Animals / also connect / memories / to feelings.

7 When / your dog / remembers / you, / it / remembers / you / are / a good person, / but / it / does not remember / when and where / you / last met.

8 This difference / is / important / because / remembering events / allows / people / to create / history.

9 We / can 'time travel' / into the past. // Can / animals / do / this? // We / do not / think / so.

02 Do You Have a Good Memory?

쉬운 독해를 위한 Vocabulary 업그레이드

A 다음 영어 표현을 읽고 뜻을 쓰시오.

1	information	_____	9	repeat	_____
2	complex	_____	10	establish	_____
3	process	_____	11	enhance	_____
4	exact	_____	12	long-term	_____
5	duration	_____	13	mind	_____
6	sentence	_____	14	store	_____
7	huge	_____	15	brain	_____
8	network	_____	16	sensory	_____

B 다음 주어진 표현을 배열하여 우리말을 영어로 쓰시오.

1 감각 기억은 우리가 보거나 듣는 것의 정확한 모방이다.

(memory / what / an exact / of / copy / we / sensory / hear / is / or / see)

2 단기 기억의 지속 시간은 보통 몇 초이다.

(a few / the duration / is / seconds / short-term / of / usually / memory)

3 장기 기억은 정보의 거대한 네트워크와도 같다.

(memory / a huge / data / of / long-term / network / is / like)

4 이것은 우리가 기억하는 모든 것을 저장한다. (the things / stores / have remembered / this / all / we)

끊어 읽기 구문 학습으로 독해 실력 업그레이드

C

다음과 같이 끊어진 표시에 유의하여 읽고, 문장을 우리말로 해석하시오.

1   Remembering information / is / one of the most complex processes / of the human brain.

2   There / are / three types of memory: / sensory, / short-term, / and long-term.

3   The brain / decides / whether / the information / is / important enough.

4   If / the information / is / important, / it / is sent / to short-term / or long-term memory.

5   If / it / is not, / it / is soon forgotten. // Sensory memory / lasts / less than a second.

6   Without this kind of memory, / we / can't work / on problems.

7   In writing an essay, / for example, / we / must be able to keep / the last sentence / in mind / as / we / write / the next.

8   Information / in short-term memory / goes into / long-term memory / when / it / is repeated / or connected with / something / we / already know.

9   Some people / believe / that / sleep / is / important / in establishing / long-term memory.

10   They / say / the process of / turning short-term memory / into long-term memory / is enhanced / during sleep.

01 More Visitors to Machu Picchu?

쉬운 독해를 위한 Vocabulary 업그레이드

A 다음 영어 표현을 읽고 뜻을 쓰시오.

1 tourist _____

2 historic _____

3 site _____

4 local _____

5 economy _____

6 limit _____

7 international _____

8 culture _____

9 realize _____

10 remain _____

11 ruins _____

12 damage _____

13 ancient _____

14 harm _____

15 environment _____

16 stone _____

B 다음 주어진 표현을 배열하여 우리말을 영어로 쓰시오.

1 페루는 더 많은 관광객을 여기로 유치하기 위해 더 열심히 노력해야 합니다.

(here / Peru / harder / should / to bring / try / more tourists)

2 그들은 여기에서 돈을 쓸 것이고, 지역 경제를 튼튼하게 만들 것입니다.

(strong / will / the local / spend / money here / they / make / economy / and)

3 관광객이 너무 많으면 고대 유물에 좋지 않을지도 모릅니다.

(may not / the old ruins / be good for / tourists / too many)

4 일부 관광객들은 환경을 해칩니다. (the environment / tourists / harm / some)

끊어 읽기 구문 학습으로 독해 실력 업그레이드

C 다음과 같이 끊어진 표시에 유의하여 읽고, 문장을 우리말로 해석하시오.

1 Some people / in Peru / want / more and more tourists / to visit / Machu Picchu.

2 What / do / you / think about / having / more visitors / to the historic site?

3 Also, / international tourists / and the local people / can learn / about each other's cultures.

4 Finally, / people / will realize / that / taking good care of / Machu Picchu / is / important.

5 I / think / Peru / should limit / the number of tourists / who / can visit / Machu Picchu / every year.

6 There / are / too many tourists already, / and / it / creates / some serious problems.

7 Visitors / can damage / the ruins / little by little.

8 Some of them / may even move / or break / some of the ancient stones. // They / leave / trash / everywhere.

9 If / more people / visit / Machu Picchu, / it / can easily turn into / an ugly place.

02 An Ancient City of Mysteries

쉬운 독해를 위한 Vocabulary 업그레이드

A 다음 영어 표현을 읽고 뜻을 우리말로 쓰시오.

1 mysterious _____

2 civilization _____

3 destroy _____

4 historian _____

5 structure _____

6 temple _____

7 fountain _____

8 blade _____

9 weigh _____

10 enormous _____

11 endanger _____

12 palace _____

13 build _____

14 become known _____

15 wheel _____

16 hundreds of _____

B 다음 주어진 표현을 배열하여 우리말을 영어로 쓰시오.

1 마추픽추는 안데스 산맥에 있는 고대 도시이다.

   (the Andes Mountains / is / an ancient city / Machu Picchu / in)

2 그곳은 세계에서 가장 아름답고 신비로운 장소들 중의 하나이다.

   (in the world / it / one of / mysterious / the most beautiful / places / and / is)

3 이 도시에는 수백 개의 석조 구조물들이 있다.

   (hundreds of / there / stone / in / are / the city / structures)

4 전 세계의 사람들이 마추픽추를 보러 찾아온다.

   (all over / Machu Picchu / people / come / from / the world / to see)

끊어 읽기 구문 학습으로 독해 실력 업그레이드

Study Date: /

C 다음과 같이 끊어진 표시에 유의하여 읽고, 문장을 우리말로 해석하시오.

1 When / the Inca civilization / was destroyed / by the Spanish, / the city / was forgotten.

2 It / became known / to the outside world / when / an American historian, / Hiram Bingham, / found / it / in 1911.

3 It / has / palaces, / temples, / parks, / fountains, / and houses.

4 Many buildings / were built / without mortar. // Blocks of stone / were cut / to fit together perfectly.

5 Some people / say / that / they / are / so perfect / that / even the blade of a knife / can't be put / between the stones.

6 Many of the building blocks / weigh / 50 tons or more.

7 How / they / moved / and / placed / enormous blocks of stone / remains / a mystery. // They / had / no horses / or wheels!

8 As / more tourists / visit / Machu Picchu, / however, / there / is / a growing danger.

9 Now / it / is / on the list / of 100 Most Endangered Sites.

A 다음 영어 표현을 읽고 뜻을 쓰시오.

1 active _____

2 volcano _____

3 alive _____

4 erupt _____

5 despite _____

6 bond _____

7 century _____

8 soil _____

9 crop _____

10 crater _____

11 harmony _____

12 remind _____

13 danger _____

14 eastern _____

15 firsthand _____

16 perhaps _____

B 다음 주어진 표현을 배열하여 우리말을 영어로 쓰시오.

1 오늘날, 수천 명의 사람들이 여전히 거기 살면서 농사를 짓고 있다.

(the land / today / farm / still live / thousands of / there / and / people)

_____

2 화산재가 토양을 농사하기에 비옥하고 좋게 만들어 준다.

(the soil / ash / and / farming / volcanic / good for / makes / rich)

_____

3 분화구 주변의 마을들은 항상 위험에 직면해 있다.

(every day / the villages / face / the crater / danger / near)

_____

4 아마도 그들은 에트나산과 조화롭게 살아가는 법을 알고 있는지도 모른다.

(Mount Etna / perhaps / in harmony with / they / live / how to / know)

_____

끊어 읽기 구문 학습으로 독해 실력 업그레이드

C   다음과 같이 끊어진 표시에 유의하여 읽고, 문장을 우리말로 해석하시오.

1   Mount Etna, / which / is / more than / 3,327 meters high, / is / Europe's highest active volcano.

2   The loud noise, / smoke, / and gas / that / come from / the mountain / remind / people / that / Etna / is / alive.

3   Despite / the dangers of this active volcano, / many people / have had / a strong bond / with Mount Etna.

4   For centuries, / people / have lived / near the mountain, / which / sits on / the eastern coast of Sicily, / Italy.

5   These people / make / money / from the large number of tourists / who / come to see / the volcano firsthand.

6   Mount Etna / is / a great place / to visit / but / not / an easy place / to live.

7   The town of Nicolasi, / just 19 kilometers / from the crater, / has been destroyed / twice.

8   The villages / near the crater / face / danger / every day. // However, / the people / have not moved away.

9   Perhaps / they / know / how to live / in harmony with / Mount Etna.

02 How Volcanoes Erupt

쉬운 독해를 위한 Vocabulary 업그레이드

A 다음 영어 표현을 읽고 뜻을 쓰시오.

1   consider _____
2   planet _____
3   crust _____
4   consist of _____
5   solid _____
6   circumstance _____
7   material _____
8   melt _____

9   underground _____
10 crack _____
11 standstill _____
12 structure _____
13 outer _____
14 form _____
15 liquid _____
16 pressure _____

B 다음 주어진 표현을 배열하여 우리말을 영어로 쓰시오.

1   중심핵은 지구의 중앙에 있으며, 고체 암석으로 이루어져 있다.

(solid rock / and / the core / at the center / consists of / of the Earth / is)

2   맨틀은 중심핵과 지각 사이에 있다. (the core / the mantle / between / is / the outer crust / and)

3   그것은 마그마라고 불리는 뜨거운 액체 암석을 형성한다.

(called / forms / magma / hot / it / rock / liquid)

4   뜨거운 가스, 화산재, 그리고 용암 때문에 화산은 강력하고 위험할 수 있다.

(powerful / becuase of / a volcano / dangerous / can be / and lava / the hot gas / and / ash)

끊어 읽기 구문 학습으로 독해 실력 업그레이드

Study Date: /

C

다음과 같이 끊어진 표시에 유의하여 읽고, 문장을 우리말로 해석하시오.

1 To understand / how / a volcano / works, / we / need to consider / the structure of the planet.

2 The Earth / has / three layers: / the core, / the mantle, / and the outer crust.

3 People / live on / the solid outer crust, / which / is / about 5 to 50 kilometers thick.

4 The largest layer, / called / the mantle, / is / between / the core / and the outer crust. // For the most part, / it / stays / solid.

5 In certain circumstances, / the mantle material / melts. // Magma / gathers / in a large underground pool.

6 When / the pressure / gets / strong enough, / a weak spot / in the outer crust / cracks, / and / the magma / shoots up / in the form of lava.

7 Tens of thousands of tourists / had to wait / for days / to get home / because / planes / stopped flying.

8 The flow of lava / and ash / also destroyed / many farms / near the volcano.

9 The eruption / brought / a lot of human activities / to a standstill.

01 An Italian-style Coffee Shop

쉬운 독해를 위한 Vocabulary 업그레이드

A 다음 영어 표현을 읽고 뜻을 쓰시오.

1 company _____

2 downtown _____

3 be impressed with _____

4 vision _____

5 create _____

6 comfortable _____

7 atmosphere _____

8 responsibility _____

9 role _____

10 society _____

11 pay attention to _____

12 fair _____

13 trade _____

14 movement _____

15 product _____

16 business _____

B 다음 주어진 표현을 배열하여 우리말을 영어로 쓰시오.

1 이탈리아의 커피 가게들은 사람들을 만나기에 아주 좋은 장소였다.

(wonderful / meeting / the Italian coffee bars / for / people / were / places)

2 그는 그의 모든 커피숍에 편안한 분위기를 만들어 냈다.

(atmosphere / a comfortable / he / all his shops / in / created)

3 스타벅스는 국내와 해외에서 빠르게 인기를 얻었다.

(became / quickly / and / both / abroad / Starbucks / popular / at home)

4 스타벅스는 이제 사회에서 그들의 역할에 대한 책임을 지려고 노력한다.

(its role / Starbucks / take / now tries to / in society / responsibility / for)

C 다음과 같이 끊어진 표시에 유의하여 읽고, 문장을 우리말로 해석하시오.

1   Now Starbucks / is / the largest coffee shop company / in the world, / with more than 28,000 stores / in 76 countries.

2   When / it / opened / in 1971, / however, / it / was / just a small shop / in downtown Seattle.

3   In 1981, / Howard Schultz / walked into / a coffee bean store / called Starbucks.

4   He / was impressed with / Starbucks' coffee / and its business, / and joined / a year later.

5   He / had / a vision / to bring / the Italian tradition / back to / the United States.

6   When / Howard / became / CEO of Starbucks, / he / put / his vision / into action.

7   Starbucks / became / a place / to meet friends, / take a rest, / read books, / enjoy music, / and / even study / or work.

8   It / uses / recycled paper cups. // It / also pays attention to / the fair trade movement.

9   It / makes sure / that / more items / on its menu / are / fair trade products.

02 Fair Trade Coffee

쉬운 독해를 위한 Vocabulary 업그레이드

A 다음 영어 표현을 읽고 뜻을 쓰시오.

1	agricultural		9	better off
2	cost		10	education
3	price		11	consumer
4	force		12	trend
5	solution		13	condition
6	profit		14	production
7	organization		15	share
8	technical		16	heath care

B 다음 주어진 표현을 배열하여 우리말을 영어로 쓰시오.

1 커피는 세계에서 가장 많이 거래되는 농산물 중 하나이다.

(in the world / the most / products / coffee / agricultural / is / one of / traded)

2 공정 무역 운동은 이 문제에 대한 한 가지 가능한 해결책이다.

(a possible solution / is / the fair / to / movement / this problem / trade)

3 공정 무역 운동은 소비자 경향이 되었다.

(trend / has become / a / the fair / consumer / movement / trade)

4 점점 더 많은 사람들이 커피 농부들의 여건에 대해 관심을 두고 있다.

(people / coffee growers / more and more / the conditions / of / care about)

C 끊어 읽기 구문 학습으로 독해 실력 업그레이드

다음과 같이 끊어진 표시에 유의하여 읽고, 문장을 우리말로 해석하시오.

1   Few people / know / that / many small coffee growers / can't even cover / the costs of production.

2   Coffee prices / in the world market / have fallen / because / large coffee companies / force / farmers / to sell / coffee / at a low price.

3   The idea / is / that / farmers / should share / in some of the profits.

4   Organizations / give / a fair trade mark / to a company / that / joins / the movement.

5   To get / this mark, / a company / must pay / the farmers / at least $1.40 / per pound.

6   It / must also lend / money / to farmers / and / give / technical help / for farming.

7   Thanks to / this movement, / more farmers / are / now better off / and / receive / health care / as well as education.

8   The fair trade movement / has become / a consumer trend. // More and more people / care about / the conditions of coffee growers.

9   Coffee lovers / are / happy / because / they / know / this fact: / the more / they / drink / coffee, / the better / the lives of the coffee growers / get.

A 다음 영어 표현을 읽고 뜻을 쓰시오.

1	satellite	9	supply
2	develop	10	repair
3	purpose	11	equipment
4	scientific	12	experiment
5	astronaut	13	investigate
6	complicated	14	benefit
7	maintenance	15	get rid of
8	unload	16	temperature

B 다음 주어진 표현을 배열하여 우리말을 영어로 쓰시오.

1 우주 비행사들은 매일 12시간씩 일한다. (a day / twelve / for / the astronauts / hours / work)

2 때때로 우주 비행사들은 수리를 하기 위해 우주선 바깥에서 일해야 한다.

(the spacecraft / have to / sometimes / to do / work outside / repairs / the astronauts)

3 우주로 나가는 것은 위험할 수 있다. (dangerous / outside / space / going / can be / into)

4 실험에서의 발견은 자연 세계에 대한 우리의 지식을 발전시킨다.

(findings / improve / the nature world / may / our knowledge / of / the research)

끊어 읽기 구문 학습으로 독해 실력 업그레이드

C   다음과 같이 끊어진 표시에 유의하여 읽고, 문장을 우리말로 해석하시오.

1   The International Space Station (ISS) / is / a large satellite / that / was developed for / the purpose of scientific research.

2   Many astronauts / from different countries / fly / to the ISS / and / stay from / a few days / to several months.

3   The ISS / is / like a large, / complicated house. // Astronauts / have to / take good care of / it.

4   Getting rid of / trash / and / unloading / fresh supplies / are / a major part of life / in space.

5   The temperature / in space / is / almost -270°C, / and / astronauts / have to move / in space / with a lot of equipment on.

6   Astronauts / also spend / much of their time / preparing / and / carrying out / scientific experiments.

7   They / investigate / the effects of / a weightless environment / on materials, / plants, / and animals.

8   The research findings / may improve / our knowledge of the natural world / and / lead / to economic / and environmental benefits.

02 **Staying Clean in Space**

쉬운 독해를 위한 Vocabulary 업그레이드

A 다음 영어 표현을 읽고 뜻을 쓰시오.

1 precious _____
2 flow _____
3 float _____
4 rinse _____
5 headache _____
6 swallow _____
7 recycle _____
8 bit _____

9 moisture _____
10 sweat _____
11 drop _____
12 at a time _____
13 bubble _____
14 dry off _____
15 toothpaste _____
16 come at a price _____

B 다음 주어진 표현을 배열하여 우리말을 영어로 쓰시오.

1 우주에서 청결을 유지하는 것은 쉽지 않다. (easy / staying / not / clean / in / is / space)

2 물이 거의 없기 때문에 모든 방울의 물이 귀중하다.

(every / little / water / drop / there / precious / is / very / is / and)

3 우주에서 양치질을 하는 것도 골칫거리이다.

(their / a headache / brushing / in / also / teeth / space / is)

4 우주 비행사들은 서로의 땀을 마실지도 모르는 것이다!

(drink / sweat / each / astronauts / may / other's)

끊어 읽기 구문 학습으로 독해 실력 업그레이드

C 다음과 같이 끊어진 표시에 유의하여 읽고, 문장을 우리말로 해석하시오.

1   Moreover, / water / does not "flow" / there, / but / "floats."

2   What / do / people / do / up there / when / they / have to stay / in the ISS / for six months / at a time?

3   To wash themselves, / astronauts / use / special soaps / and shampoos / which / do not need / water / to rinse.

4   They / must use / the soaps / carefully. // If / they / don't, / the soap bubbles / will go / all over / the place.

5   After / washing, / they / use / a towel / to dry off.

6   Astronauts / use / toothpaste / and toothbrushes / just like the ones / on Earth, / but / there / is / no sink / in the spacecraft.

7   After / brushing / their teeth, / astronauts / have to swallow / the toothpaste.

8   Even the moisture / in sweaty clothes / is taken out / and / recycled for / drinking / and other purposes.

9   Does / living in space / still sound / great? // Don't forget / that / it / comes / at a price.

01 Louis Pasteur's Great Work

쉬운 독해를 위한 Vocabulary 업그레이드

A 다음 영어 표현을 읽고 뜻을 쓰시오.

1	terrible		9	bite
2	disease		10	deadly
3	matter		11	career
4	survive		12	experiment
5	inject		13	scientific
6	protect		14	solution
7	vaccine		15	heat
8	mad		16	safe

B 다음 주어진 표현을 배열하여 우리말을 영어로 쓰시오.

1 파리에서 끔찍한 질병이 많은 양과 소를 죽였다.

(in Paris / cows / disease / many / killed / a terrible / sheep / and)

2 Louis Pasteur는 그 문제를 면밀하게 살펴보고 흥미로운 점을 발견했다.

(something / Louis Pasteur / the matter / and / found / looked into / interesting)

3 그 동물들은 절대 그 끔찍한 질병에 걸리지 않았다.

(disease / the animals / caught / the terrible / never)

4 Pasteur는 질병에 맞서는 백신을 발견했던 것이다.

(a vaccine / Pasteur / found / the disease / against / had)

C

끊어 읽기 구문 학습으로 독해 실력 업그레이드

다음과 같이 끊어진 표시에 유의하여 읽고, 문장을 우리말로 해석하시오.

1 If / an animal / survived / the disease, / it / never caught / that / disease again.

2 If / I / inject / a weak form of the disease / into healthy animals, / they / will be protected.

3 One day / in 1885, / a doctor / brought / a boy / to Pasteur. // The boy's name / was / Joseph Meister.

4 A mad dog / had bitten / him, / so / the doctor / thought / he / would get / a deadly disease / called / rabies.

5 The doctor / took / the boy / to Pasteur / because / he / was experimenting with / a rabies vaccine.

6 Though / Pasteur / had never tried / it / on people, / he / decided to try / his vaccine / on the boy anyway.

7 During / Pasteur's career, / he / found / many scientific solutions / to everyday problems.

8 One of the other problems / was / milk. // People / could catch / diseases / from it.

9 Pasteur / found / that / if / he / heated / the milk, / it / became / safe / and / could keep / it / longer / than before.

02 How Vaccinaions Work

쉬운 독해를 위한 Vocabulary 업그레이드

A   다음 영어 표현을 읽고 뜻을 쓰시오.

1 injection _____

2 moment _____

3 contain _____

4 stimulate _____

5 immune system _____

6 prevent _____

7 fight off _____

8 vaccination _____

9 painful _____

10 save _____

11 cause _____

12 enough to _____

13 antibody _____

14 enter _____

15 formation _____

16 develop _____

B   다음 주어진 표현을 배열하여 우리말을 영어로 쓰시오.

1 우리는 아프지 않기 위해서 주사를 맞는다. (to be / get / sick / injections / we / not)

2 고통스러운 한순간이 우리가 많은 질병에 걸리는 것을 막아준다.

(moment / diseases / one / getting / from / painful / us / keeps / many)

3 과학자들은 많은 다른 질병에 대한 백신들도 개발할 수 있을 것이다.

(develop / diseases / may / scientists / many / for / be able to / vaccines / other)

4 백신 덕택에 사람들은 더 오래, 더 건강한 삶을 살고 있다.

(lives / thanks to / people / live / vaccines / healthier / longer)

C 다음과 같이 끊어진 표시에 유의하여 읽고, 문장을 우리말로 해석하시오.

1 We / get / injections / when / we / are / sick. // These injections / are called / vaccinations.

2 In fact, / vaccinations / are / the main reasons / why / people / live / longer / these days.

3 Vaccines / contain / forms of bacteria / and viruses / which / cause / diseases.

4 These bacteria / and viruses / are called / pathogens. // Pathogens / in vaccines / are not / strong enough / to cause / diseases.

5 When / we / get / a vaccination, / weak pathogens / are injected / into the body.

6 They / stimulate / the immune system, / which / makes / antibodies.

7 The formation of these antibodies / is / the key / to preventing diseases / in the future.

8 These antibodies / will remember / how to kill / the pathogens.

9 When / strong pathogens / enter / the body, / the antibodies / will help / our body / quickly fight / them off.

10 Scientists / have developed / vaccines / for diseases / such as small pox, / chicken pox, / measles, / and malaria.

쉬운 독해를 위한 Vocabulary 업그레이드

A 다음 영어 표현을 읽고 뜻을 쓰시오.

1	celebrate		9	tradition
2	predict		10	indicate
3	last		11	severe
4	hibernate		12	belief
5	shadow		13	settler
6	frighten		14	adopt
7	retreat		15	dig
8	method		16	believe

B 다음 주어진 표현을 배열하여 우리말을 영어로 쓰시오.

1 Groundhog Day는 북아메리카에서 잘 알려진 기념일이다.
(holiday / North America / is / a well-known / Groundhog Day / in)

2 겨울에 그라운호그는 곰처럼 겨울잠을 잔다.
(a bear / the winter / hibernates / like / a groundhog / in)

3 그것은 굴속으로 다시 들어가 봄을 기다린다.
(retreat / spring / it / its hole / wait for / will / and / into)

4 이주민들은 후에 그라운드호그를 날씨 예보자로 삼았다.
(later adopted / their / the groundhog / the settlers / weather predictor / as)

끊어 읽기 구문 학습으로 독해 실력 업그레이드

C 다음과 같이 끊어진 표시에 유의하여 읽고, 문장을 우리말로 해석하시오.

1 It / is celebrated / in the United States / and Canada / on February 2.

2 According to / the weather of the day, / people / predict / whether / the cold winter / will last / longer / or / the warm spring / will soon come.

3 A groundhog, / also known / as a woodchuck, / is / a small animal / that / digs / a hole / and / lives / under the ground.

4 It / is said / that / the groundhog / wakes up / from its hibernation / and / comes up / from its hole / on February 2.

5 If / it / is / sunny, / the groundhog / will see / its shadow / and / be frightened.

6 If / it / is / cloudy, / it / will not see / its shadow. // Then, / it / will stay / above the ground.

7 Many Americans / watch / the sky / on February 2 / and / they / are / happy / if / it / is / cloudy. // Spring / is / near!

8 This method of weather prediction / came from / the European tradition of Candlemas, / which falls / on February 2 / as well.

9 This belief / was brought to / America / during the 18th century / by German settlers.

02 **Spring Celebrations**

쉬운 독해를 위한 Vocabulary 업그레이드

A 다음 영어 표현을 읽고 뜻을 쓰시오.

1	ancient	___	9	custom	___
2	hardship	___	10	assimilate	___
3	differ	___	11	reach	___
4	gift	___	12	ritual	___
5	myth	___	13	symbol	___
6	contain	___	14	decorate	___
7	source	___	15	national	___
8	destroy	___	16	grave	___

B 다음 주어진 표현을 배열하여 우리말을 영어로 쓰시오.

1 전 세계의 사람들은 언제나 봄이 오는 것을 기념해 왔다.

(the coming of / people / have always / around the world / spring / celebrated)

2 고대인들에게 봄은 새로운 희망과 새 생명의 시간이었다.

(spring / new life / and / a time of / ancient peoples / new hope / was / for)

3 사람들은 부활절에 달걀을 장식하고 먹는다.

(eat / people / Easter Day / decorate / and / eggs / them / on)

4 이날 이후로 낮이 밤보다 길어지기 시작한다.

(the nights / after / become / that day / the days / than / longer)

끊어 읽기 구문 학습으로 독해 실력 업그레이드

Study Date: /

C

다음과 같이 끊어진 표시에 유의하여 읽고, 문장을 우리말로 해석하시오.

1 When / the hardship of winter / finally retreated / and / spring / came, / they / celebrated.

2 While / customs / differed / in different places, / many people / thought / the egg / a symbol of new life / or rebirth.

3 The ancient Egyptians / and Persians / celebrated / spring festivals / by painting / and / eating / eggs.

4 In ancient Russia, / eggs / were given / as gifts / in springtime.

5 According to / a Russian myth, / the egg / contained / a source of fire / that created everything.

6 Many of these customs / were assimilated into / the Christian Easter celebration.

7 The early Christians / adopted / the egg / as a symbol of / the resurrection of Jesus Christ.

8 Many cultures / hold / spring celebrations / on the spring equinox, / which / usually falls / around March 20.

9 In Japan, / it / is / a national holiday, / when / families / get together / and / visit / their family graves.

01 Who Invented the Elevator?

쉬운 독해를 위한 Vocabulary 업그레이드

A 다음 영어 표현을 읽고 뜻을 쓰시오.

1	transparent	9	attack
2	primitive	10	enemy
3	operate	11	convey
4	waterwheel	12	demonstrate
5	device	13	freight
6	describe	14	equip
7	raise	15	increase
8	weapon	16	confidence

B 다음 주어진 표현을 배열하여 우리말을 영어로 쓰시오.

1 승강기는 우리 주변 어디에나 있는 것 같다. (around / seems / all / are / it / us / elevators)

2 그것들은 커다란 돌덩이처럼 무거운 물체를 들어 올리기 위해 사용되었다.

(of / heavy / like / blocks / were used to / big / lift / objects / stone / they)

3 원시적인 승강기는 기원전 3세기만큼이나 일찍 사용되었다.

(the 3rd / primitive / as early as / elevators / century BC / were / in use)

4 전기 승강기는 수십 년 후에 사용되기 시작했다.

(use / decades / electric / came into / elevators / later / several)

끊어 읽기 구문 학습으로 독해 실력 업그레이드

Study Date: /

C

다음과 같이 끊어진 표시에 유의하여 읽고, 문장을 우리말로 해석하시오.

1 Modern elevators / are / amazing. // In one hotel / in Germany, / for example, / you / can go up / and down / in a fish tank.

2 The elevator / is / in the middle / of a tube / of water / containing / many sea animals.

3 If / glass walls / are not / enough, / try / Sky Tower / in New Zealand.

4 It / takes / you / straight / to the top / in 40 seconds / – on a transparent floor!

5 Like / many other inventions, / however, / elevators / started out / simple.

6 It / was used / to raise / a large weapon / to attack an enemy.

7 They / were / platforms / operated by / human, / animal, / or waterwheel power.

8 From / the mid-19th century, / power elevators, / often steam-operated, / were used for / conveying materials / in factories, / mines, / and warehouses.

9 In 1853, / American inventor / Elisha Otis / demonstrated / a freight elevator / equipped with / a safety brake / to prevent / falling / in case / a supporting cable / breaks.

02 Up, Up and Away

쉬운 독해를 위한 Vocabulary 업그레이드

A 다음 영어 표현을 읽고 뜻을 쓰시오.

1 science fiction _____

2 predict _____

3 reality _____

4 lifetime _____

5 announce _____

6 realize _____

7 inefficient _____

8 multiple _____

9 require _____

10 fuel _____

11 contrast _____

12 impossible _____

13 countless _____

14 imagine _____

15 international _____

16 unrealistic _____

B 다음 주어진 표현을 배열하여 우리말을 영어로 쓰시오.

1 일본의 한 회사는 2050년까지 우주 승강기를 만들 계획을 발표했다.

(announced / by 2050 / one / in Japan / to make / plans / company / a space elevator)

2 많은 사람들이 로켓 여행이 얼마나 비효율적인지 알지 못한다.

(inefficient / people / is / don't / travel / realize / many / how / rocket)

3 로켓은 우주를 여행하는 데에 가장 좋은 방법이 아닐 수도 있다.

(space / may not be / way / to get / the best / rockets / into)

4 사람들은 케이블에 매달려 그들 사이를 오르내리며 여행하는 것이다.

(them / travel / a cable / people / up and down / on / between)

끊어 읽기 구문 학습으로 독해 실력 업그레이드

C 다음과 같이 끊어진 표시에 유의하여 읽고, 문장을 우리말로 해석하시오.

1   Imagine / sitting / in an elevator car, / riding far up / into space / on a cable.

2   Actually, / many scientists / predict / that / space elevators / will become / a reality / within our lifetime.

3   In 2018, / elevator experiments / started / at the international space station.

4   First of all, / rockets / can hold / only a few people / or objects, / and / only some of them / can be used / multiple times.

5   They / also require / a lot of fuel. // This / means / that / getting into space / with a rocket / costs / a great deal.

6   In contrast, / elevators / can be used / again and again / without as much fuel.

7   There / is / a space station / on one end / and Earth / on the other.

8   Then / remember / what / people / used to say / about flying / in the air.

9   Yet, / today, / countless people / fly / in airplanes / every day.

01 **Sharing Books with People**

쉬운 독해를 위한 Vocabulary 업그레이드

A 다음 영어 표현을 읽고 뜻을 쓰시오.

1 somewhere _____

2 pick up _____

3 practice _____

4 share _____

5 stranger _____

6 release _____

7 log on _____

8 register _____

9 note _____

10 go hunting _____

11 identification _____

12 community _____

13 interesting _____

14 for free _____

15 benefit _____

16 save _____

B 다음 주어진 표현을 배열하여 우리말을 영어로 쓰시오.

1 당신이 책을 어딘가에 놓아둘 수 있다. (somewhere / you / books / leave / can)

2 그것들은 다른 사람들에 의해 주워지고 읽힌다.

(be picked up / others / they / and / read / by / may)

3 이 네트워크에 가입하는 것은 간단하다. (network / to / is / simple / it / this / join)

4 회원들은 자신들의 지역에 방출된 책을 찾으러 웹사이트를 검색할 수 있다.

(search / books / members / the website / can / in / for / their area / released)

끊어 읽기 구문 학습으로 독해 실력 업그레이드

C 다음과 같이 끊어진 표시에 유의하여 읽고, 문장을 우리말로 해석하시오.

1 There / is / an interesting way / to take care of / the books / you / don't need / anymore.

2 This practice of "BookCrossing" / was started / by Ron Hornbaker / in the U.S. / in 2001.

3 He / created / the website bookcrossing.com, / which / helps / people / share / books / with friends / and even total strangers.

4 To leave / or "release" / a book / somewhere, / log on / to the website / and / register / the book. // Note / where and when / it / will be released, / and then / go out / to release / it.

5 A person / who / picks up / a book / must visit / the website.

6 He or she / must enter / the book's identification number / and information / about where and when / it / was picked up.

7 After / it / has been read, / the book / should be released / again / for someone else / to read.

8 Become / a part of this community of / readers. // There / are / several benefits / to BookCrossing.

02 Teens and Fantasies

쉬운 독해를 위한 Vocabulary 업그레이드

A   다음 영어 표현을 읽고 뜻을 쓰시오.

1   survey _____

2   require _____

3   novel _____

4   fantasy _____

5   translate _____

6   fascinate _____

7   appeal _____

8   character _____

9   inspire _____

10 mythology _____

11 imagination _____

12 allow _____

13 explore _____

14 escape _____

15 language _____

16 stressful _____

B   다음 주어진 표현을 배열하여 우리말을 영어로 쓰시오.

1   어떤 사람들은 오늘날 십 대들이 책을 전혀 읽지 않는다고 생각한다.

(some / that / these days / think / teens / at all / don't read / people)

2   소설, 특히 판타지는 전 세계적으로 십 대들 사이에서 인기 있다.

(the world / are / among / novels / around / teens / popular / especially fantasies)

3   그것들은 수십 가지의 언어로 번역되었다.

(languages / they / dozens of / have been / into / translated)

4   난 신문이나 잡지는 읽고 싶지 않아요. (reading / don't / magazines / feel like / I / newspapers / or)

끊어 읽기 구문 학습으로 독해 실력 업그레이드

C 다음과 같이 끊어진 표시에 유의하여 읽고, 문장을 우리말로 해석하시오.

1 A recent survey of U.S. teens / shows / that / almost 43% of them / read / for fun / in their free time.

2 This means / that / many teens / do reading / that / is not required / for schoolwork.

3 C. S. Lewis's *Chronicles of Narnia* / and J. K. Rowling's *Harry Potter* books, / for example, / top / the lists of teens' favorite books.

4 Why / are / teens / so fascinated / with fantasies?

5 The answer / lies / in the fact that / the genre itself / is appealing / to teens.

6 In a fantasy, / anything / can happen, / and / there / are / cool characters.

7 Stories / are / often inspired / by mythology; / the stories / are full of / magic and events / that / are / possible / only in the imagination.

8 So, / a good fantasy / allows / people / to easily forget / about the stressful real world / and / explore / an exciting, imaginary one.

9 Fantasies / are / a perfect escape / for teens / who / are looking for / a way to relax.

01 Names Around the World

쉬운 독해를 위한 Vocabulary 업그레이드

A 다음 영어 표현을 읽고 뜻을 쓰시오.

1 custom _____
2 culture _____
3 official _____
4 cradle _____
5 circumstance _____
6 refer to _____
7 unique _____
8 term _____
9 compose _____
10 syllable _____
11 sibling _____
12 common _____
13 vary _____
14 basket _____
15 based on _____
16 instead _____

B 다음 주어진 표현을 배열하여 우리말을 영어로 쓰시오.

1 아기 이름을 짓는 풍습은 문화마다 다르다.

(naming / vary / customs / for / cultures / across / babies)

2 바구니는 아기를 넣는 요람이다. (is / a baby / for / a basket / holding / a cradle)

3 많은 말레이시아인들은 성이 없다. (don't / family / many / names / have / Malays)

4 한국에서 대부분의 사람들은 두 음절로 된 이름을 갖고 있다.

(have / in Korea / most / two syllables / a given name / people / composed of)

끊어 읽기 구문 학습으로 독해 실력 업그레이드

C 다음과 같이 끊어진 표시에 유의하여 읽고, 문장을 우리말로 해석하시오.

1 In the African-American Gullah community, / for example, / babies / are given / both / an official name / and a basket name.

2 The basket name / is usually chosen / based on / the circumstances of the baby's birth.

3 If / a child / was born / on a Friday, / its basket name / could be / Friday.

4 Within the community, / people / refer to / each other / by their basket names, / and / often don't know / each other's official names.

5 Another unique naming custom / is found / in Malaysia.

6 Instead, / men / add / their father's name / to their own name / with the term "bin," / which / means / "son of."

7 On the other hand, / women / use / the term "bint," / which means / "daughter of."

8 For example, / brothers / Kim Jeong-min / and Kim Jeong-su / share / the syllable "jeong" / in their given names.

9 However, / this practice / is becoming / less common.

UNIT 11

02 John Who?

쉬운 독해를 위한 Vocabulary 업그레이드

A 다음 영어 표현을 읽고 뜻을 우리말로 쓰시오.

1 village _____
2 neighbor _____
3 surname _____
4 population _____
5 record _____
6 tricky _____
7 suppose _____
8 tax _____

9 collector _____
10 toward _____
11 occupation _____
12 characteristic _____
13 personal _____
14 tell apart _____
15 create _____
16 choice _____

B 다음 주어진 표현을 배열하여 우리말을 영어로 쓰시오.

1 마을에 여섯 명의 John이 있다고 가정해 보라.

(were / the village / suppose / there / Johns / in / six)

2 어떤 사람들은 그들이 사는 곳에 근거하여 성을 지었다.

(created / lived / some / they / people / where / based on / surnames)

3 다른 사람들은 직업에 근거하여 성을 지었다.

(occupations / surnames / their / based on / created / others)

4 많은 성이 개인의 특성에서 취해졌다.

(personal / many / taken / characteristics / were / from / surnames)

44 · UNIT 11

C 끊어 읽기 구문 학습으로 독해 실력 업그레이드

C 다음과 같이 끊어진 표시에 유의하여 읽고, 문장을 우리말로 해석하시오.

1 Until the early years / of the Middle Ages, / most people / in Europe / lived / in small farming villages.

2 Everyone / knew / their neighbors, / and / there / was / little need / for last names / or surnames.

3 As / the population / and / the towns / grew, / however, / record keeping / became / tricky.

4 How / was / the tax collector / to make sure / which ones / had paid / their taxes?

5 So, / people / needed to find / ways / to tell apart / people / who / shared / the same first name.

6 If / one / lived / toward the east, / "Easter" / was / a perfect choice.

7 For example, / someone / who / baked / bread / for a living / called / himself / "Baker."

8 If / one / had / brown hair, / "Brown" / served as / a good surname.

9 "Bright" / and "Smart" / are / also surnames / based on / personal characteristics.

UNIT 12

01 The Most Famous Painkiller

쉬운 독해를 위한 Vocabulary 업그레이드

A 다음 영어 표현을 읽고 뜻을 쓰시오.

1 painkiller _____ 9 chemical _____

2 history _____ 10 compound _____

3 bark _____ 11 familar _____

4 willow _____ 12 tablet _____

5 chemist _____ 13 invention _____

6 discover _____ 14 date back to _____

7 element _____ 15 tough _____

8 relieve _____ 16 suffer from _____

B 다음 주어진 표현을 배열하여 우리말을 영어로 쓰시오.

1 아스피린은 고대로부터 중요한 진통제였다.

(has been / times / aspirin / since / an important / ancient / painkiller)

2 사람들은 인류에게 더 이상 고통이 없을 것이라고 생각했다.

(thought / would be / human beings / people / there / for / pain / no more)

3 버드나무의 살리신은 위에 부담을 주었다.

(stomachs / from / tough / willow / salicin / on / plants / was)

4 아스피린의 발명은 곧 1920년대 전 세계적인 확산으로 이어졌다.

(the 1920s / soon led to / spread / the invention / its worldwide / in / of aspirin)

끊어 읽기 구문 학습으로 독해 실력 업그레이드

C 다음과 같이 끊어진 표시에 유의하여 읽고, 문장을 우리말로 해석하시오.

1 The history of aspirin / dates back to / Hippocrates, / the ancient Greek physician / who / lived sometime / between 460 BC and 377 BC.

2 He / used / powder / from the bark / and / leaves of the willow tree / to take care of / headaches, / pains, / and fevers.

3 By 1829, / chemists / discovered / that / the element / called salicin / in willow plants / helped / relieve / pain.

4 In 1853, / French scientist Charles Frederic Gerhardt / found / a way / to solve / the problem.

5 In 1897, / German chemist Felix Hoffmann / came up with / a more efficient method / and / gave / it / to his father / who / was suffering / from arthritis.

6 The resulting compound / received / its familiar name of aspirin / in 1899.

7 Aspirin / was sold / as a powder / before / the first aspirin tablets / were made / in 1915.

8 Throughout / the 20th century, / many uses / for aspirin / were found.

9 Aspirin / is now being used / to reduce / swelling, / ease heart problems, / and relieve arthritis.

02 How the Placebo Effect Works

쉬운 독해를 위한 Vocabulary 업그레이드

A

다음 영어 표현을 읽고 뜻을 우리말로 쓰시오.

1 drug ____________

2 effective ____________

3 take part in ____________

4 experiment ____________

5 placebo ____________

6 result ____________

7 compare ____________

8 researcher ____________

9 response ____________

10 demonstrate ____________

11 prescribe ____________

12 ethical ____________

13 claim ____________

14 deceive ____________

15 get better ____________

16 be related to ____________

B

다음 주어진 표현을 배열하여 우리말을 영어로 쓰시오.

1 신약이 효과가 있는지를 어떻게 알 수 있을까?
(effective / how / is / do / drug / we / a new / know / whether)

2 어떤 연구자들은 그 효과가 마음에서 온다고 믿는다.
(the mind / some / comes from / believe / researchers / that / the effect)

3 의사들은 오랫동안 속임약을 사용해 왔다.
(ages / doctors / for / placebos / have / used)

4 그들은 의사들이 환자들을 속인다고 주장한다.
(claim / the patients / deceive / they / that / doctors)

끊어 읽기 구문 학습으로 독해 실력 업그레이드

C 다음과 같이 끊어진 표시에 유의하여 읽고, 문장을 우리말로 해석하시오.

1 Usually, / two groups of people / take part in / an experiment.

2 One group / is given / the new drug, / whereas / the other group / is given / a placebo.

3 A placebo / is / a pill / that / looks / exactly the same / as the new drug / but / is not / real medicine.

4 Later, / the results / from the two groups / are compared / to see / whether / the new drug / has been / effective.

5 Surprisingly, / about one-third of people / got better / thanks to / placebos. // This / is called / the placebo effect.

6 According to / this theory, / people's trust / in a placebo / helps / them / feel well / and / ultimately get better.

7 More than half of doctors / in the U.S. / regularly prescribe / placebos, / such as vitamins, / to help / their patients.

8 Some people / think / that / the practice / is not / ethical. // They / claim / that / doctors / deceive / the patients.

9 Others, / however, / don't see / anything wrong / with doctors / prescribing them.

UNIT 13

01 Bring Images to Life

쉬운 독해를 위한 Vocabulary 업그레이드

A 다음 영어 표현을 읽고 뜻을 쓰시오.

1 entertainment _____

2 excitement _____

3 offer _____

4 still _____

5 sequence _____

6 photograph _____

7 create _____

8 lifelike _____

9 animator _____

10 necessary _____

11 be capable of _____

12 passion _____

13 realize _____

14 a series of _____

15 nevertheless _____

16 skilled _____

B 다음 주어진 표현을 배열하여 우리말을 영어로 쓰시오.

1 만화 영화는 20세기 초에 처음 등장했다.

(in the early / the animated / appeared / 20th century / cartoon / first)

2 매년 만화 영화가 전 세계에서 큰 인기를 얻는다.

(animated / the world / every year / are / cartoons / big hits / around)

3 이 정지 이미지들은 한 장면 안에서 매우 빠른 속도로 보인다.

(a squence / the still / a very fast / images / in / are shown / at / rate)

4 특수 카메라가 그 결과를 찍는 데 사용된다.

(the results / camera / is used / a special / to photograph)

C   다음과 같이 끊어진 표시에 유의하여 읽고, 문장을 우리말로 해석하시오.

1   Since then, / many people / have enjoyed / this type of entertainment.

2   Movie-goers of all ages / are fascinated by / the excitement / that / animated cartoons / offer.

3   Few realize, / however, / that / an animated cartoon / is / only a series of "still" images.

4   As many as / 24 images / are shown / per second. // Together, / the images / appear / to be moving.

5   A still image / is called / a frame. // There / are / two main ways / to make frames.

6   In one way, / images / are drawn / and then / photographed / to make frames.

7   The other way / is / to make / use of a model frame. // A model frame / is made / and / changed / in small ways.

8   An animated cartoon / needs / a huge number of frames, / so / it / wasn't / easy / to produce / a good one.

9   Thanks to / computer technology, / however, / it / is / now easier / to create / lifelike characters / using special software.

02 Enjoy An Animation Festival

쉬운 독해를 위한 Vocabulary 업그레이드

A 다음 영어 표현을 읽고 뜻을 쓰시오.

1 celebrate _____

2 anniversary _____

3 opportunity _____

4 adult _____

5 hatter _____

6 curse _____

7 ashamed _____

8 castle _____

9 promise _____

10 imprisoned _____

11 set free _____

12 separate _____

13 penniless _____

14 turn into _____

15 come across _____

16 homeless _____

B 다음 주어진 표현을 배열하여 우리말을 영어로 쓰시오.

1 네 편의 애니메이션이 하루에 상영될 예정입니다.

(different / the same / cartoons / are going to / on / be shown / four / day)

2 당신이 애니메이션을 사랑하는 사람이라면 이 기회를 놓치지 마세요.

(a cartoon / don't / this / miss / if / lover / are / you / opportunity)

3 캘시퍼는 소피가 저주를 풀도록 도와주겠다고 약속한다.

(promises / the curse / her / break / Calcifer / to help)

4 그녀는 갇혀있는 요정 진에 대한 마법 같은 이야기를 아이들에게 들려준다.

(them / Djinn Fairy / she / magical stories / tells / of / the imprisoned)

C 다음과 같이 끊어진 표시에 유의하여 읽고, 문장을 우리말로 해석하시오.

1 Candle Cinema / is celebrating / its thirtieth anniversary / with cartoons / from around the world.

2 Four different cartoons / are going to be shown / on the same day.

3 Sophie, / a hatter, / is cursed by / the Witch of the Waste, / and / turns into / an old woman.

4 Along the way, / she / comes across / Howl's moving castle.

5 Ashamed of / how / she / looks, / she / decides to / run away.

6 Inside the castle, / Sophie / meets / the fire demon Calcifer / whose work / is making / the castle / move around.

7 White-skinned, / blue-eyed / Azur / and dark-skinned, / brown-eyed / Asmar / are raised / as brothers / by Asmar's gentle mother.

8 She / tells / them / magical stories of / the imprisoned Djinn Fairy / waiting / to be set free.

9 Azur / is sent away / to study, / while / Asmar / and his mother / are driven out, / homeless / and penniless.

UNIT 14

01 Home Remedy for Snoring

쉬운 독해를 위한 Vocabulary 업그레이드

A

다음 영어 표현을 읽고 뜻을 쓰시오.

1 snore	______	9 attach	______
2 painful	______	10 breathe	______
3 cause	______	11 nasal	______
4 vibration	______	12 strip	______
5 tissue	______	13 throat	______
6 muscle	______	14 lie	______
7 passage	______	15 roommate	______
8 comfort	______	16 position	______

B

다음 주어진 표현을 배열하여 우리말을 영어로 쓰시오.

1 어떻게 하면 제 룸메이트가 코를 골지 않게 할 수 있을까요?
(keep / snoring / how / my roommate / do / I / from)

2 코골이는 인후에 있는 세포 조직의 진동 때문에 일어납니다.
(caused by / the tissues / vibrations / snoring / his throat / of / is / in)

3 코 테이프는 그가 이러한 방법으로 숨을 쉬는 것을 배우게 도와줄 것입니다.
(learn / way / a nasal / help / will / to breathe / this / strip / him)

4 그러면 그는 입으로 숨 쉬는 것을 막을 수 있습니다.
(will / mouth / then / through / his / stop / he / breathing)

끊어 읽기 구문 학습으로 독해 실력 업그레이드

C 다음과 같이 끊어진 표시에 유의하여 읽고, 문장을 우리말로 해석하시오.

1 My roommate Jake / is / a good guy, / but / he / snores / like a motorbike.

2 Every night / I / try to / fall asleep / before / him. // If / I / fail, / I / will have / painful hours / before / I / can sleep.

3 When / he / sleeps / on his back, / the tissues / in the throat / slide back / as / the muscles / relax.

4 As / air / moves through / the passage, / the tissues / vibrate, / causing / the snoring sounds.

5 Dr. Cureall / is / right. // People / snore / when / they / sleep / on their backs.

6 Here / is / a great way / to keep / your roommate / from sleeping / on his back.

7 When / he / lies / on his back, / it / will give / enough discomfort / to change / his sleeping position.

8 A nasal strip / will / help / him / learn to breathe / this way. // The strips / will open up / his nose / so more air / comes in.

A   다음 영어 표현을 읽고 뜻을 우리말로 쓰시오.

1   wonder _____

2   trimmer _____

3   filter _____

4   nasal _____

5   average _____

6   germ _____

7   lung _____

8   purpose _____

9   humidity _____

10   respiratory _____

11   attack _____

12   infection _____

13   cautious _____

14   clip _____

15   trap _____

16   maintain _____

B   다음 주어진 표현을 배열하여 우리말을 영어로 쓰시오.

1   당신은 왜 코털이 있는지 궁금하게 여겨본 적이 있는가?

(wondered / why / nose / you / ever / have / we / hair / have)

2   그것은 우리의 건강을 유지하는 데 중요한 역할을 한다.

(us / plays / keeping / it / healthy / an important / in / role)

3   코털은 코의 통로에서 여과기 역할을 한다.

(passages / nose / a filter / works / as / hair / our / nasal / for)

4   습기는 호흡기 계통에 중요하다. (important / system / humidity / is / respiratory / for / your)

끊어 읽기 구문 학습으로 독해 실력 업그레이드

C 다음과 같이 끊어진 표시에 유의하여 읽고, 문장을 우리말로 해석하시오.

1   It's / definitely not / for decoration / or for the benefit of makers / of nose hair trimmers.

2   A person / breathes / in an average of / 10,000 liters / of air per day.

3   When / you / breathe in / air / through your nose, / you / are breathing / in the germs, / fungus / and dust / in the air, too.

4   It / keeps / them / from entering / your lungs / and making / you / sick.

5   Another purpose / of nose hair / is / to maintain / the humidity level / of the nasal passages.

6   It / provides / heat and moisture / when / you / breathe in / air / and / traps / humidity / when / you / breathe out.

7   Without nose hair, / your throat / would be / dry / and your lungs / wouldn't work / properly.

8   Overgrown nose hair / may not be / good / to see, / but / it / should never / be removed / completely.

9   Without nose hair, / you / are / more likely to / get / colds, / allergy attacks / and other infections.

01 The Oldest Snack Food

쉬운 독해를 위한 Vocabulary 업그레이드

A 다음 영어 표현을 읽고 뜻을 쓰시오.

1	dough	_____	9	form
2	unique	_____	10	fold
3	knot	_____	11	prayer
4	loop	_____	12	reward
5	twist	_____	13	consider
6	strip	_____	14	market
7	develop	_____	15	become known
8	monk	_____	16	fat-free

B 다음 주어진 표현을 배열하여 우리말을 영어로 쓰시오.

1 이것은 긴 원통형의 밀가루 반죽으로 만들어 구운 음식의 일종이다.

(of / a type / dough / long rolls / from / made / baked food / is / it / of)

2 최초의 프레츨은 어떻게 만들어졌을까? (into / how / being / pretzel / the first / come / did)

3 어느 날 그는 빵을 만들고 반죽이 남았다.

(making / one day / left / bread / dough / he / some / had / over / after)

4 그는 이 프레츨을 기도를 배우는 아이들에게 줄 선물로 썼다.

(used / learned / who / the pretzels / as treats / for kids / their / he / prayers)

끊어 읽기 구문 학습으로 독해 실력 업그레이드

C

다음과 같이 끊어진 표시에 유의하여 읽고, 문장을 우리말로 해석하시오.

1 A pretzel / is / a popular snack / in Europe / and North America.

2 It / has / a unique shape: / the knots / and loops / are made / by twisting / the strips of dough.

3 How / did / the first / pretzel / come into being? // Nobody / knows / for sure.

4 Many people, / however, / say / the pretzel / is / the oldest snack food / ever developed.

5 According to / some scientists, / the pretzel / was first developed / in the early 7th century / by a monk / in southern France / or northern Italy.

6 He / formed / the pretzel shape, / which / looked like / a child's arms / folded / in prayer.

7 He / called / the snacks / "pretiola," / which / means / "little reward" / in Latin.

8 The pretiolas / found / their way / into Germany / and Austria, / where / they / became known / as pretzels.

9 The pretzel market / has grown / in recent years / because / pretzels / are considered / a healthy, / fat-free snack.

02 What Makes Bread Rise?

쉬운 독해를 위한 Vocabulary 업그레이드

A 다음 영어 표현을 읽고 뜻을 쓰시오.

1 ingredient _____

2 flour _____

3 bubbly _____

4 yeast _____

5 rise _____

6 fungus _____

7 single-celled _____

8 organism _____

9 microscope _____

10 multiply _____

11 environment _____

12 carbon dioxide _____

13 puff up _____

14 knead _____

15 distribute _____

16 evenly _____

B 다음 주어진 표현을 배열하여 우리말을 영어로 쓰시오.

1 빵 반죽은 안에 이스트가 있어서 부푸는 것이다.

(rises / the yeast / the bread / it / because / dough / in / of)

2 1그램에는 20억 개의 이스트 세포가 들어 있다!

(yeast / 20 billion / one gram / contains / of / yeast cells)

3 이것은 습기 찬 환경에서 당을 섭취하면 빠른 속도로 증식한다.

(rapidly / when / a moist / it / environment / eats / multiplies / sugar / in / it)

4 왜 어머니는 빵 반죽을 치댈까? (the bread / mother / does / your / dough / why / knead)

끊어 읽기 구문 학습으로 독해 실력 업그레이드

C 다음과 같이 끊어진 표시에 유의하여 읽고, 문장을 우리말로 해석하시오.

1 How / can / simple ingredients / like flour, / sugar, / salt, / and eggs / produce / wonderfully bubbly bread?

2 It / is / the work of the yeast, / which / creates / soft, / tasty bread.

3 Without yeast, / your bread / would be / too hard / for you / to even chew.

4 Yeast, / a kind of fungus, / is / a single-celled organism / that / can be seen / only through a microscope.

5 Though / it / is / tiny, / yeast / is / a living thing / that / can grow / or die.

6 It / multiplies / rapidly / when / it / eats / sugar / in a moist environment.

7 It / dies / when / it / is / too cold / or too hot. // This / is / why / warm water / is used / to make / bread dough.

8 As / the yeast / eats / the sugar, / it / produces / carbon dioxide / and other chemicals.

9 Kneading the dough / helps distribute / the yeast cells evenly / throughout the dough.

10 Kneading / also helps / carbon dioxide bubbles form / in the dough.

A 다음 영어 표현을 읽고 뜻을 쓰시오.

1	burst	9	palace
2	embroider	10	speechless
3	anticipation	11	fling
4	humble	12	deeply
5	beloved	13	handsome
6	wound	14	surface
7	return	15	cruelty
8	fisherman	16	teacup

B 다음 주어진 표현을 배열하여 우리말을 영어로 쓰시오.

1 그녀는 강에 뜬 낚싯배로부터 노래를 들었다.

(from / she / a fishing / heard / the river / boat / in / a song)

2 근처 마을에서 어부를 데려왔습니다. (a nearby / we / from / a fisherman / village / brought)

3 그의 가슴 위에는 커다란 수정이 놓여 있었다. (a large / on / sat / chest / his / crystal)

4 그녀의 방은 그의 달콤한 노랫소리로 가득 찼다. (his / filled / sweet / room / her / with / song)

C 끊어 읽기 구문 학습으로 독해 실력 업그레이드

다음과 같이 끊어진 표시에 유의하여 읽고, 문장을 우리말로 해석하시오.

1 The princess / spent / most of her time / in her room / at the top of the tower, / reading / or embroidering.

2 "How / beautiful / the song / is! // The man / who / can sing / such a beautiful song / must be / young / and handsome."

3 From that day on, / the princess / waited / by the window / to hear / the song again.

4 As / time / went by, / her anticipation / changed into / a broken heart. // She became / pale / and weak.

5 "You / must find / the handsome young man / who / sang / this song," / said / the maid, / and sang / it.

6 Seeing / the fisherman, / the king / was / speechless.

7 The fisherman / was brought to / the princess's room / and / sang / the song.

8 As soon as / she / heard / the song, / the princess / jumped from / her bed / and / got dressed.

9   Instead of / a young / and handsome prince, / there / stood / a humble-looking / fisherman.

10   She / turned / her head away / and / said, / "Close / the door."

11   The fisherman / was sent / home. // But / he / could hardly eat / or sleep.

12   He / had fallen / in love. // He / grew ill.

13   In a few days, / the villagers / found / him / dead / in his hut.

14   "It / is / his heart," / the wise old woman / in the village / said.

15   "The princess / wounded / him / so deeply, / his heart / turned hard / to stop / the pain."

16   The villagers / put / the crystal / in the fisherman's boat / and / pushed / it / to the river.

17   Just as / she / was about to drink, / she / saw / the fisherman's face / on the surface of the tea.

18   She / remembered / her own cruelty. // "What / have / I / done? // I'm / so sorry."

헉!

내 성적의
비밀에는
이유가 있어

기본 탄탄 나의 첫 중학 내신서
체크체크 전과목 시리즈

국어
공통편·교과서편/학기서

모든 교과서를 분석해 어떤 학교의
학생이라도 완벽 내신 대비

수학
학기서

쉬운 개념부터 필수 개념 문제를
반복 학습하는 베스트셀러

사회·역사
과학
학기서/연간서

전국 기출 문제를 철저히 분석한
학교 시험 대비의 최강자

영어
학기서

새 영어 교과서의 어휘/문법/독해
대화문까지 반영한 실전 대비서

조금 더
공부해
볼까?

배움으로 행복한 내일을 꿈꾸는
천재교육 커뮤니티 안내 . . .

 교재 안내부터 구매까지 한 번에!
천재교육 홈페이지

자사가 발행하는 참고서, 교과서에 대한 소개는 물론
도서 구매도 할 수 있습니다. 회원에게 지급되는 별을 모아
다양한 상품 응모에도 도전해 보세요!

 다양한 교육 꿀팁에 깜짝 이벤트는 덤!
천재교육 인스타그램

천재교육의 새롭고 중요한 소식을 가장 먼저 접하고 싶다면?
천재교육 인스타그램 팔로우가 필수!
깜짝 이벤트도 수시로 진행되니 놓치지 마세요!

 수업이 편리해지는
천재교육 ACA 사이트

오직 선생님만을 위한, 천재교육 모든 교재에 대한 정보가 담긴
아카 사이트에서는 다양한 수업자료 및 부가 자료는 물론
시험 출제에 필요한 문제도 다운로드하실 수 있습니다.

https://aca.chunjae.co.kr

 천재교육을 사랑하는 샘들의 모임
천사샘

학원 강사, 공부방 선생님이시라면 누구나 가입할 수 있는 천사샘!
교재 개발 및 평가를 통해 교재 검토진으로 참여할 수 있는 기회는 물론
다양한 교사용 교재 증정 이벤트가 선생님을 기다립니다.

 아이와 함께 성장하는 학부모들의 모임공간
튠맘 학습연구소

튠맘 학습연구소는 초·중등 학부모를 대상으로 다양한 이벤트와 함께
교재 리뷰 및 학습 정보를 제공하는 네이버 카페입니다.
초등학생, 중학생 자녀를 둔 학부모님이라면 튠맘 학습연구소로 오세요!